MAMA DEVOW

THE DEVIL'S CONCUBINE

Mama Devow
The Devil's Concubine

Rhoan Flowers

* 2021 Rhoan Flowers... All rights reserved

No part of this book may be reproduced, distributed, stored in a retrieval system, or transmitted by any means, including photocopying, recording, or other electronic or mechanical methods, without the prior written permission of the author, except in the case of brief quotations embodied in critical reviews and certain other non-commercial uses permitted by copyright law.

ISBN: 978-1-989995-04-4 (P.C)
ISBN: 978-1-989995-05-1   (E.C)

Library and Archives of Canada
395 Wellington Street
Ottawa, Ontario

Be advised, any websites mentioned in this publication may have changed since book release.

The StreetAuthor

Introduction

Throughout the centuries, humans have visited practitioners of sorcery for a number of reasons. Some people had absolutely no trust in modern medicine and thus sought the assistance of Bush Doctors or Herbal Healers as alternatives to curing whatever ailments they suffered. For individuals interested in joining a demonic organization, there was none more powerful than Obeah, which was an ancient technique used to communicate with spirit forces from the Dark Realm. The practice originated in Africa and was used in the Caribbean for the first time by a slave girl who grew up to become the first Obeah Queen of Westmoreland. Members of the Obeah Religion lived by a strict code of conduct and sincerely worshiped the Lord of the Underworld, whose mission was to increase his congregation and capture more human souls.

After discovering that her daughter was slated to become the next Obeah Queen of the West Indies, Daliah Devow began making preparations to smuggle away the child to a foreign land where she could live a normal life instead. Their slave ancestor had entered an everlasting binding contract with the Lord of the Underworld, who gained worshippers for his congregation in exchange for supernatural powers and wealth. Because of this unethical contract, an heir to the presiding Obeah Queen was born every hundred years before ascending to the throne at the age of 19.

Madam Dion Devow who ruled over the estate had several aliases such as The West Witch, Mama Devow, Obeah Worker and Bush Doctor to name a few. Nothing that pertained to the witch's estate transpired without her consent, therefore she had ample knowledge of the plot to smuggle away her successor and allowed it to happen. However, in order for their family legacy to survive the heir to the Devow Estate had to be present at the time of Dion's retirement to receive the transfer of power. Everyone assumed that the Obeah Queen was only interested in her successor as a replacement, but Dion was rather scrupulous and had other ideas on who should manage the Devow Estate. To bring her successor back to Jamaica the West Witch assembled a team and sent them to kidnap the female, but what surprises awaited the witch or the members of her abduction team?

Chapter 1

The sounds of thunder rumbled across the night's sky as raindrops smashed against the zinc rooftop, which had tiny holes throughout that caused drips of water to trickle into the house. The residents placed five cooking pots, a bucket, a clothing wash pan, a kettle, two large soup bowls and a juice jug all throughout the interior of their home to catch the intrusive rainwater. There were still a few unattended holes where rainwater fell to the floor, because they had nothing else with which to contain it. Daliah Devow and her boyfriend Tyliq Davis were submerged beneath their sheets cautiously engaged in coitus, inside their single room house. The overwhelming sexual stimulation caused the young stallion to groan continuously, against which his companion argued that "their daughter was still sound asleep!" Both partners were utterly captivated by each other as they clutched tightly and enjoyed the intimacy, until Tyliq climaxed and passed out in Daliah's arms.

The dwelling in which they lived was barely big enough for two and the mattress on which they slept was the only other seat apart from two chairs underneath a small table, therefore their young daughter had no choice but to sleep beside them on the bed. The couple lived in a wooden house built along the main road used by travelers commuting through the district of Mount Carey in the parish of St. James, Jamaica. The house originally belonged to Daliah's father who passed away and left her the structure, hence she and her boyfriend made it their home. Throughout the community not many families had the luxury of electricity or interior plumbing, thus much of those who had light illegally bridged current from the city's main power lines. There outhouse bathroom and toilet facilities were built approximately ten yards away from the house, but they had to travel to the standpipe up the hill to fetch clean water.

Like most houses on the hillside the couple's single room dwelling was anchored by a pair of 8 foot, 8x8 wooden planks; with the entrance located to the rear to avoid the additional lumber needed to construct a step. There was a single window built with wooden panes instead of glass at the front of the house, which overlooked the main road approximately thirty yards down the steep hill. The paint on the outside of the residence had all but vanished, exposing the bare wood's cracks and flaws. Despite the physical appearance of the house the structure was sound and had endured many thunderstorms and hurricanes, but the impoverished young dwellers were simply happy to have a place of their own. The community pathway that led from the base of the road up to the top of the hill ran close by the couple's door, therefore, someone was often strolling by despite the hour of the day.

At 2:54 A.M. the six-months-old baby started fussing and awoke the young mother who quickly attended to the child to avoid disturbing her partner who had to wake early for work. The little baby, who had made significant strides that resulted in her sleeping through the night, was very irritated and refused to calm down even after her mother changed her nappy and soothingly cuddled her. While breast feeding the infant, the child's father who was sound asleep sat up and rose from the bed, then proceeded to walk over to the front door, unlatched it and opened it with his eyes still firmly shut as if he expected company.

THE DEVIL'S CONCUBINE

"Tyliq what you doing," jokingly asked the young mother who had never observed her boyfriend sleepwalking?

The young father who was still sound asleep neglected her questioning and stood holding the door ajar for some twenty seconds before an old woman walked into the residence. The breast-feeding mother, who had grown concerned for her boyfriend's health and their safety, placed the baby on the bed and was moving towards Tyliq when the unexpected intruder entered. There were two lazy mongrel dogs living in the adjacent yard that seldom barked at anyone who passed, thus Dahlia wondered how it was that she got by without exciting them. The presence and sight of the intruder sent a bone-chilling sensation through the already nervous female, hence she pretended as if she wasn't intimidated and became vociferous.

"Is who you and why you walking into people's house at this hour? Old lady you better get your ass out my house before I get vex you hear me," said the young mother!

"Shut your mouth child," stated the old woman as she waved her staff before the female's face!

Instantly Daliah froze and could only manage to rotate her eyes to see what was transpiring inside their home, as if she had been drugged with some sort of crippling concoction. Tyliq had closed the door and stood like a centurion sound asleep, so she feared for their lives and wondered what were the intruder's intentions? The audacious old woman who was dressed like a native African wearing a long black robe, a black turban cloth that wrapped her dreadlocks and black sandal on her feet, walked past the female and went over to the infant laying on the bed. With what only could be determined as malice, the unwelcomed female grabbed the adorable infant by the left leg, brought her to the center of the room and tossed her on her back on the wooden floor. There were white markings all over the intruder's face like an African Warrior who wore face paint into battle and hand paintings like those on an Indian bridge. The old woman also carried a black pouch from which she proceeded to remove several artifacts then placed them beside the baby, used a white chalk to draw a circle around the child, lit candles and laid an ancient medallion directly on the child's forehead. Without any direct instruction, the old lady snapped her fingers at which Tyliq walked over to the lamp on the table and extinguished the light, before returning to his prior position. Daliah frantically looked on through the corners of her eyes as the intruder finally withdrew a pointed dagger and placed it in front of her and then began some sort of demonic ceremony.

The immobilized female watched and listened as the old woman chanted in another language for several minutes, before she said a prayer to the one she worshiped and swayed from side to side with both eyes firmly closed. Daliah could not believe what she was witnessing as the woman drifted off into a trance. The intruder, after a few tranquil minutes, suddenly stopped and started trembling during which her eyes popped open glistening red like blood, as she ripped off the infant's clothing, grabbed for the dagger and started carving an exact replica of the symbol featured on the medallion in the center of the girl's chest. The tormented mother could hear herself screaming for help at the top of her lungs but not a single word uttered from her mouth, hence she fell unconscious under the overwhelming duress.

The audacious intruder drained the sprinkled blood from her dagger into a small tube, then placed them both gently into her pouch. Suddenly as if shocked with a jolt of lightening the mystical old woman's fingers extended fully, wherein she slowly passed both hands over the baby's wounds and instantly healed them. The intrusive old woman picked up the child and returned her to bed, then collected the rest of her belongings and telepathically transferred some instructions to the man of the house. Tyliq remained sound asleep throughout the entire ordeal, as he showed the intruder out and closed the door behind her, then transferred Daliah to her bed. Before laying back down, Tyliq also cleaned up the mess left by the Obeah woman, and ensured that there was no evidence of her being there.

After such an eventful night the female was awakened a few hours later by her boyfriend's rumblings as he prepared to leave for work. The young mother awoke in a state of shock and franticly looked around the room as if there was some sort of demonic presence inside the dwelling, before she grabbed for her baby daughter who was sound asleep and held her tight.

"You look like you had a bad dream," stated Tyliq as he shoved his feet into his shoes!

THE DEVIL'S CONCUBINE

"Are you sick or something, you don't remember the old creepy woman last night," argued Daliah?

"Ha-ha-ha-ha, you mean that I had you seeing old people last night? That's a new one," responded Tyliq, as he grabbed his groin and did some provocative antics.

"Please don't flatter yourself! But I'm not joking, is you open the door and let her in," said Daliah!

"Sounds more like you drop off the bed and hit your head last night. Anyways I have to go so I see you later," answered Tyliq.

Daliah reached for her cellular phone and dialed a long-distance number at which she discovered that she hadn't enough credits available to make the call. The baby's nappy was wet and the young mother sought to change her before she ran out to the local shop to purchase the items she needed. As soon as she unfastened the child's sleeper Daliah froze with astonishment at the sight of the strange symbol carved into her daughter's chest, moreover she was even far more fascinated with the healing process used. To ensure that the baby sustained no further injuries the mother checked her thoroughly, before they both dressed and left the house.

On her way down to the main road Daliah passed the elderly woman next door stooped over a huge pan of laundry, which was a chore she did twice weekly by thoroughly hand washing each piece of clothing and placing them on a clothesline in the sun. The night's rain had caused the pathway to become slippery and muddy, therefore the young mother had to be extremely careful going down. The Old Woman noticeably watched Daliah walk down the slippery pathway, then immediately used her cellular and made a phone call.

The local shop was within a five-minute walk down the main road and as soon as Daliah got to the base of the hill, she ran into a neighbor known as Helen who was heading in the same direction. There was a single road lane heading in either direction that was separated by only the center marking; and without constructed sidewalks so the ladies had to walk in the bushes and rubbles along the roadside to avoid getting struck by passing motorists. Regardless of the treacherous and narrow winding roads, cars, motorcycles, buses, trucks and trailers sped along as if they were competing in the Indy 500 race. Both ladies had recently given birth to baby girls and thus immediately started chatting about the trials of motherhood, during which Daliah revealed the incident that occurred the night prior.

To prove her point Daliah securely held her baby across her arm and unbuttoned two of her sleeper's top buttons to show the carved symbol, but there was absolutely nothing for Helen to see. The female neighbor thought that the pressures of motherhood and being alone throughout the day was beginning to affect Daliah and excused her delusional claims. The symbol's disappearance caused Daliah to become more adamant about the situation, to which she argued "that someone was trying to play tricks on her." While approaching the wooden shop Daliah who was by then suspicious of everything and everyone noticed a motorist cruising by in a Nissan Sunny who blatantly stared at her.

After acquiring their merchandise, both ladies were walking back home when, two minutes into their stroll, the same vehicle that passed before crept up behind them and started cruising slowly at a distance. The disturbance in the flow of traffic caused irate drivers to honk their horns in protest, before shouting various sorts of profanity at the driver once they were able to pass his car, yet still he cruised at a snail's pace behind the young mothers. Both ladies soon observed the stalking vehicle and walked faster to safety reach their destination. As soon as Daliah reached the pathway that led up to her home the pursuing vehicle sped up and flew by, however both ladies were able to get a proper view of the driver's face as he stared at them. Daliah exchanged parting sentiments with her neighbor and scurried up the hill to her home, where she was overwhelmingly nervous that someone might follow her.

The instant she got home Daliah bolted the latch on the door, placed the baby on the bed, turned on their small television and pressed play on her favorite Barney DVD. The young mother then tapped up the credits on her cellular phone and placed the call she originally intended. The intrusion that transpired terrified the young female, thus she telephoned the only person she knew capable of helping. Dahlia felt afraid in her own house for the first time since she lived there, to the extent that every rattle of the boards caused her to twitch or jump. To allow more lighting to enter the room the female opened the window and looked through at the beautiful scenic view, but the sight of the same Nissan Sunny vehicle parked at the base of the hill forced her to quickly reclose it.

"Hello honey how is the baby," responded the call receiver after the telephone rang the third time!

"Remember when you told me that if anything abnormal happens to let you know right away," said Daliah?

"Did something happen," enquired the female on the phone?

"Mom I'm so scared I think that I'm losing my mind! Last night Tyliq sleepwalked to the door and opened it for this old woman. Then she walked right in and this morning I find some marking on Danielle's chest," cried Daliah into the phone!

"Slow down baby you're going too fast, now describe the marking to me," asked the mother?

"You didn't just hear what I said about Tyliq sleepwalking and opening the door," enquired Daliah?

"Yes, I did but this is way more important, now what does the symbol look like!?"

"It look like some Chinese drawing but I think I've seen this sign before somewhere or in a dream," Daliah emphasized.

"Probably when you were a baby, one day I was forced to bring you to see this old lady. That is all I can tell you for now but don't mention any of this to anyone else," whispered the mother!

"But how did she manage to get Tyliq to open the door in his sleep," argued the sobbing female who picked up the baby and held her close to her bosom?

"Your boyfriend is one of her servants now, she don't only control him but she can also see everything that him see," answered the mother.

"How is that possible and who is this old woman anyways," enquired Dahlia?

"It's not who she is so much as what she is, and she is first and foremost your great-grandmother. Never forget that," exclaimed her mother!

"Then this morning when I walked to go down a shop this weird guy followed me there and back and as soon as I reached home him speed off down the road! But now I think him come back once again! What should I do I'm so afraid," added Dahlia?!

"You have been marked, so she go keep using all her servants to watch your every move. From now on you have to be cautious! Don't worry, none of them can cause you any harm. I have some good friends that helped me to escape from the island that I go call and try to get them to help us," Instructed the mother.

"Well, no relative of mine is going to treat my child like she did and I consider us still related," said Dahlia!

"This only stays between us you understand! I'm going to try to get you to come away and live with me until we sort this matter out, but this have to be done in secrecy or we'll never be successful. Now remember, not a single word to a soul no matter what," assured her mother!

Chapter 2

The old woman who entered the couple's house unannounced got chauffeured back to her home in the Savanna La Mar district, situated south of Mount Carey along Route 86. The area was still under the cloud of night when the woman, born Dion Devow, but most popularly known as "The West Witch," arrived home in her Cadillac hearse driven by her personal chauffeur. The West Witch, who was revered throughout the district lived on a twenty acres' piece of property in a vintage European-style house that was still as elegant as the day it was constructed. Residents in the community would often refer to Madam Devow's house as the White House of Savanna La Mar, because of the glistening white paint and the structure's resemblance to that of the American monument. There was a female maid present to open the car door once the vehicle pulled up at the front of the house, with a pleasant greeting as if she had not seen the lady of the house in ages. All of Madam Devow's servants were very well attired and spoke proper English when referring to her, however it was indeed evident that they were utterly terrified of her. None of her servants or the people with whom she dealt dared to stare her in the eyes when addressing her, as if she was royalty amongst whom peasants were warned not to gaze upon and to keep their heads bowed.

Dion Devow was the most powerful Obeah practitioner in the Caribbean who provided a mystical service to those who sought such assistance. The West Witch provided a list of services to her clients, such as mental and physical health healing, vengeance seeking, demonic protection, the acquisition of wealth and fame and many other unnatural requests. A majority of the contracts entered with the witch were only payable by the surrendering of one's soul to the Devil at the time of their death. Regardless of what was stipulated in each deal, every client of the West Witch eventually got added to her global network for the remainder of their existence. The Devow family had been rooted in the Savanna La Mar region since the days of slavery and grew to become the most powerful family throughout the district. Even the local Jehovah's Witnesses abstained from visiting or even passing by Madam Devow's property, hence rumors circulated that the Obeah practitioner casted a spell that deterred certain people from coming close to her residence. The old woman's personal clients referred to her as Mama Devow and believed strongly in her gift. She rarely accepted new clients, and it was incredibly difficult to get an appointment to sit with her. The Obeah practitioner produced such startling results that people would travel from far overseas for an hour of her council, therefore she had a waiting list of clients that had more standbys than most physicians.

Madam Devow's estate was estimated to be worth a whopping two hundred million pounds, which made her the richest female in the parish. Her first client that morning was an American billionaire who was diagnosed with terminal cancer and advised by his physicians that 'he only had two months left to live' as the cancer had spread to his brain. In his quest to lengthen his life expectancy Mr. Riley placed an advertisement in the infamous New York Times Magazine for a magical cure and received several inquiries, but none of them corresponded after he sent them his current diagnosis. The failing-health billionaire was with his physicians in his hospital room one day, when he suddenly picked up the phone which only rang inside his head and answered it. The voice on the line instantly hypnotized Mr. Riley and only gave him an address to the West Witch's house in Savana La Mar. None of the doctors present heard the phone ring, therefore, they all speculated that their patient might be experiencing some form of Dementia, however Mr. Riley finished his call and immediately arranged for the hospital's helicopter to bring him to the airport. Against the recommendations of his doctors, the billionaire decided to travel abroad and alerted his travel service for them to prepare his jet.

That morning was the billionaire's 84th fourth visit since his doctor's diagnosis and at five thousand American dollars per visit he wasn't about to quit and prove his former physicians' theory. The maid was on hand to open Mama Devow's client's rear passenger door once he arrived in his S 500 Benz, before she led him into the Healing Chamber where Madam Devow awaited him. The room had black paint on the walls and ceiling with drawings of skeletons and other African symbols done in white paint throughout the room. There were black marble tiles across the floor, glistening as if they had been polished and shined with lit candles in placeholders on every wall that illuminated most of the room. The light failed to reach all four corners inside the room which brought an eerie feeling as if there were others present. Without an actual request, the client removed an envelope containing the funds necessary to honor their arrangement from his pocket and gave it to the maid, who politely thanked him with a bow before walking backwards from the room. The Obeah woman's assistant left the room and sealed the door with several deadbolt locks, to ensure that the spirits invoked in the practice stayed inside the chamber.

"Morning to you Mama Devow," exclaimed the visitor!

"Welcome back Mr. Riley, as customary, remove your clothing and lay on the cot," instructed the old woman who had her back turned while preparing the concoction necessary to perform her task!

Mr. Riley who had been visiting his unorthodox healer at 8:00 A.M every morning for the past two plus months was only dressed in his robe, whereby he simply removed it and hung it on a metal hook and lay down naked on the cot. The sound of a Rastafarian Nyabinghi Drum beating in the background was a ritual whenever Mama Devow engaged in her

Obeah sessions, but none of her patients knew from where the sounds came. The lit candles around the chamber were the only source of lighting and the cot placed in the center of the room gave the appearance of an operating facility minus the surgical equipment. Jasmin incents were used to mask a foul stench similar to that of a rotting corpse that came from an open fireplace, but the smell didn't provoke either of the occupants.

To begin, Madan Devow brought a piece of wooden peg and placed it between her client's teeth for him to bite tightly onto. The removal of cancerous cells from one's body without surgically extracting the venom was an incredibly painful procedure that lasted for some two hours each visit, during which the patient was completely conscious and observed the poisonous chemicals being extracted. The entire treatment was estimated to take between six to twelve months during which the client was advised not to miss any appointment, as they gradually reduced the life-threatening cancer tumors. The Black Arts Practitioner had not fully reached halfway through her treatment and Mr. Riley was already way more active than he had been over the past two years, had regained most of the weight he lost and had also began experiencing hair regrowth.

There were two ways to extract the cancer cells from one's body and those were either by urinating or defecating the substance that would leak out with a texture similar to black oil. The procedure required that Madam Devow rub an ointment onto Mr. Riley's skin while chanting in tongues. The ointment was left to soak into the pores for five minutes during which the witch would dance around in a trance, while puffing on a huge cigar and then exhaled the residue on her patient. Within seconds after inhaling the fumes from the ointment Mr. Riley became dizzy and felt more relaxed, which allowed the Obeah practitioner to operate more freely. With her patient properly sedated the witch retrieved some preheated black stones that were kept warm inside the fireplace and placed them beside the cot, before ensuring they weren't too hot to apply to her client's skin. The room was by then filled with steam and felt like a warm sauna as Madam Devow slowly ran her hands over her client's body, until she came to an area where the cancer cells caused her to begin shaking uncontrollably. Wherever she sensed a quantity of the life-threatening cells she would immediately cover the area with heated rocks, which slowly melted away the cancer cells and caused the toxins to drain from the body. The draining process was incredibly painful because of the thick leaking substance involved, but after being drugged Mr. Riley was so relaxed that he simply smiled and bit on the peg.

As each treatment session neared its end, a pig was let into the chamber through a secret hatch. The West Witch insisted that the animal 'was necessary to ingest the dangerous spirits that exited with the cancerous cells or they would find an alternate host to enter and infect.' Mama Devow would mix the small amounts of cancerous fluids that drained from Mr. Riley each day with some sort of food item and feed it to the animal. The pig was the only creature on earth capable of digesting and entrapping such toxic entities, which, if not contained, could have easily sickened and killed it. Mr. Riley was strong enough to leave immediately after every session, although he initially staggered about as if he was impaired off liquor.

***

After Mr. Riley departed, Madam Devow would customarily rest for 45 minutes until her second patient for the day arrived, but that morning while she rested an unexpected visitor came to see her. The unscheduled visitor was Cynthia Clark, a local resident who had recently gotten divorced and was forced to return to the work force to fend for herself and her daughter, who was born with Down Syndrome, which confined her to a wheelchair. Prior to the departure of her husband, Cynthia would care for their daughter each day while he went off to work and provided for the family. Sexual tensions and other problems caused the husband to cheat and eventually run off with his mistress, leaving his wife to struggle to fend for herself and their 14-year-old child. The family lived off Hudson Street in an area of town that was relatively safe, but it had been reported that crime was on the rise throughout the region.

Cynthia had a number of troubling issues with which to contend, and was at the point where she wanted some compensation for the terrible issues she had been tackling. The single mother was scheduled to be at work that morning, but unless she dealt with her problems, she knew that she would sustain a nervous breakdown. Fear was the primary factor why most people in town abstained from passing near the West Witch's property, hence for Cynthia the walk felt like a condemned prisoner heading to the death chamber. The single mother walked up to the front door and banged the brass doorknocker three times and patiently waited for someone to respond.

"Good morning, how may I help you," responded the maid?

"Good morning, I know I don't have an appointment, but I would like to speak with the lady of the house please," answered Cynthia?

"I'm sorry but I'm afraid that this is her relaxing…," began the maid before she was interrupted by her mistress who was walking down the staircase.

"Show Miss Clark in Barbara," instructed Madam Devow!

"Yes ma'am! You may enter and follow me please," said Barbara as she closed the door then led the way!?

Even though the house was spectacularly grand and exquisite with rich and beautiful furniture, statues and artwork, very little sunlight was allowed inside the structure, so it was difficult to see the unique antiques. Cynthia was led into the Counselling Room that was filled from wall to wall with ancient books, where the mistress stood flipping through the pages of a very rare publication.

"Speak your request Miss Cynthia Clark," insisted Madam Devow!

"I can't take no more Madam Devow! My husband run off with some young gal and leave me all alone to watch for our special needs child. Since him leave I have to work and go to school over five months now; and I just recently find out that my handicap daughter pregnant and I don't even know by who," declared Cynthia as she wondered to herself how it was that the witch knew her name!?

"I feel the hatred in your heart, but tell me what is it that you want," questioned Madam Devow?

"The doctors them say she past four months so she can't get an abortion. We barely have enough for us two so I can't afford another mouth to feed, I'm begging you for something to make this pregnancy go away? Whoever raping my child when I gone to work during the day,

THE DEVIL'S CONCUBINE

I want their penis to rotten like an old willow tree! As for my cheating ass ex-husband, make him turn impotent like the day him born, and I want his worthless ass to pay to help protect and take care of his daughter… who is getting molested because I'm not there to watch her a daytime," broke down and cried the single mother!

The Obeah Woman went over to a secretive cabinet built into the wall and opened the huge doors revealing hundreds of ointments in small bottles. Madam Devow selected a specific potion and measured out a small amount, then threw the contents into a plastic bag and passed her visitor the package, which Cynthia collected and shoved inside her purse.

"When you get home this evening throw half of this in a glass with half cup of Coconut Water and give your daughter to drink tonight, and the other half in the morning, and by the afternoon she go get her period! Pay the little money you have to Barbara and I want you to return tomorrow with some hair from your ex-husband old brush and by then I'll have something to help get rid of the rapists then," instructed the Obeah Practitioner!

Upon her departure, Cynthia was surprised to see a local police squad car pulling into the visitor's designated parking spot, nevertheless she dragged her handbag over her shoulder and briskly walked away. The driver of the squad car was Madam Devow's next client, therefore Barbara stood patiently by the door as he made his way in.

***

"Good day Officer Thompkins the Madam is awaiting you inside the reading room," stated the maid as she closed the door then led the way.

Madam Dion Devow awaited her client inside the same chamber she saw Mr. Riley earlier, wherein her maid collected the officer's clothes before departing and sealing the entrance. The mistress of the house stood beside the cot and instructed the officer to lay on his back, before she secured his arms and legs with leather straps attached underneath the cot. Constable Glen Thompkins was a rookie officer at the Savanna La Mar Police Department, and a local resident who was born and raised in the district. The peaceful town of Savanna La Mar had drastically increased in crime over the past few years and the young rookie was determined to change the culture back to that of years past. The street bangers involved in crime saw the police department as a group of old countrymen who were incapable of protecting the district, therefore crime was at an all-time high with new gangs emerging from different areas and an Influx of heavy weaponry.

An incident occurred three weeks before where Officer Thompkins and his partner Constable Slay Flemings were walking through the downtown market, when they came across two known gunmen in the process of collecting sales tax from all the market vendors. Constable Thompkins first noticed the commotion where the vendor who was incapable of paying was getting assaulted in addition to his merchandise being vandalized. His partner who had stopped to chat with a female he knew eventually caught sight of what was transpiring and rushed to intervene before matters escalated. By the time Constable Fleming, a 31-year-veteran of the police force made his way through the gathered crowd and reached the conflict, he undoubtedly missed the slap that flung his partner's head around and nearly dislocated his jaw, but the echo from the contact was too loud to miss. Officer Thompkins was so shocked by getting slapped across his face that he started grabbing for his gun, which led both extortionists to begin retracting for their weapons. At the sight of weapons being drawn the crowd started dispersing as patrons feared getting unintentionally shot.

"Yow you guys just cool man! Officer Glen put away your service weapon, you don't want no argument with these guys," shouted Constable Fleming as he leapt in the middle of the argument! "Bully, Ferro, him new to the police force give him a chance man. I will fill him in on how things run around here! No need for any bloodshed today gentlemen!"

"Make sure you warn your boy Fleming, cause next time them go have to clean him up off the tar," Bully threatened!

Even though Constable Thompkins was scared shitless, he could not believe the audacity of his partner from whom he expected support in his attempt to conduct official police business. Officer Thompkins was tempted to shoot the thugs despite having his partner between the gunmen and himself, because he was utterly embarrassed and could only hear the ramblings of witnesses who were beginning to mock him. The Young Rookie holstered his weapon with tears bobbled in his eyes and a burst of laughter from the crowd; and vowed from that moment to never again allow a criminal to get the better of him. Regardless of what his partner explained thereafter Officer Glen was irate at the fact that gunmen drew their weapons at him and walked away without injury, but he would never forget their faces and struggled from that day to quench his thirst for vengeance.

Madam Devow was rumored to have performed some of the most impractical devilish acts within the district, therefore the rookie officer privately visited her for help in achieving the self-confidence and psychiatric bravery required to perform his duties adequately. The Obeah Lady who prayed before engaging in all of her demonic practices, said a few words to her master before commencing the ceremony. Officer Thompkins' hands and feet were then bound to the cot with leather straps and buckles to keep them firmly secure. Another pair of leather straps were used to hold Officer Thompkins' head and body firm against the cot, as the sounds of Mama Devow's African drums started slowly beating in the background. The Obeah woman began slowly chanting in tongues as the drumbeats consumed her to where she began dancing and parading like a folk dancer around the chamber. There was a fireplace that could be closed with a decorative sectional that was open and during her trance-like rampage the West Witch threw a small vile containing some clear fluid inside. A small flame ignited and burnt with a blue light without the assistance of any wood or petroleum substance, as Madam Devow attended to the client and danced around him during which she blew some powdery chemicals directly in the officer's face. The instant Constable Thompkins breathed in the dust particles he began sneezing prior to feeling a weird sensation as if he had been drugged.

Even though the officer chose to undergo the procedure, the terrifying process was one that often-caused participants to develop second thoughts, which was why they had to be securely tied to the cot. Once the drummer started beating more rapidly the fire inside the fireplace changed colors from blue to red and grew immensely in size, to the extent that spirit forces began hurling from the flames and circled the room. Mama Devow had opened a portal between hell and earth from which some of the evilest souls to ever walk this planet came through.

MAMA DEVOW

The trained officer believed that he was experiencing hallucinations until one of the spirits floated directly above him and lingered there with a blank stare, through which Glen saw nothing but unmentionable catastrophes, death and decay. Aside from the visions of destruction the officer could clearly hear Mama Devow loudly summoning someone from the depths of hell, before which the Devil's grand champion answered and came forth.

As the evil spirit travelled through the portal and made its way into the modern realm the entire room rumbled and felt like an earthquake erupting. Every other spirit that floated about the chamber departed and flew back into the flames the instant the summoned spirit materialized. It then stood before Madam Devow and conversed with her for nearly 20 seconds. At the end of their discussion Madam Devow simply told Glen to "open his mouth" and without quarrel the hypnotized officer did as instructed. Constable Thompkins had never experienced that level of paranoia as he stiffened his entire body and tightly clinched his ass-cheeks and widened his eyes as the spirit circled the room then flew directly into his body orally. Instantly the flame inside the fireplace extinguished and Madam Devow froze with her eyes closed, before she regained consciousness and freed the officer from his bondages. Officer Glen Thompkins who was quite aware of what happened to him, rose from the cot and politely bowed his head thanking the madam, then walked out as the chamber doors opened.

***

Throughout the duration of that day, Madam Devow saw eight other clients: a public eye figure, whose lovely wife was cheating with another man, an ambivalent female who was jealous of her friend and sought to put a curse on her. There was also the son of a 76-year-old developer who wanted his father dead, a young entertainer seeking wealth and fame in the music industry, three superstitious females who regularly visited to have their futures predicted by getting their palms read and a paid assassin who wanted paranormal protection. The West Witch who rarely slept would see clients up till 11 PM, but occasionally performed personal after hour duties.

Chapter 3

Being the parent of a special need's child is especially difficult without the help of the other parent or a government program, thus for Cynthia receiving word that her daughter had qualified for a subsidized handicap program was the second good news she got the day following her visit with Madam Devow. The excited mother returned home after another hard day's work plus evening classes to find her handicapped daughter Grace naked on the floor after the youths who seldom raped her left her as such. The single mother had reported every known incident to the police, who could do very little to prevent the crime from reoccurring because of the location of their home. The house was situated about 80 yards' inlet off Hudson Street, which was the main roadway through the town and could not be seen by the police officers who routinely patrolled the area. The officers at the station could only provide recommendations to help Cynthia, but she could not afford the high-tech gadgetry that were quoted. Officers also suggested that Cynthia purchase burglar bars for her windows and doors or even get a guard dog, but neither suggestions were within her budget.

The bedrooms inside Cynthia's home were located to the back of the house, hence it was also impossible for her closest neighbor, an elderly woman who lived with her son and two granddaughters, to see or hear anything. The old woman would generously check on Grace at least twice daily during which she fed the crippled teenager and ensured she had enough drinking water inside her water bottle. Cynthia's gracious neighbor was the person who uncovered those responsible for molesting Grace, when she unexpectedly went by the house one day. When the youths heard the neighbor entering, they ran through the back door to escape, but she caught a glimpse of them as they fled. There weren't any homes built behind Cynthia's house and the undeveloped land beyond her property allowed for anyone to wonder by unseen. The doctors at the hospital had managed to collect sperm samples from her daughter the few times she brought her there following an attack; and officers were eager to get the results in order to locate and arrests whoever was responsible for the despicable crime.

The single mother would rush her daughter to the General Hospital regardless of how tired she was, but things would be different on this night. With tears flowing down her face Cynthia rushed to her daughter's aide wherein she helped her into her wheelchair and brought her into the bathroom. One of Cynthia's newest methods to save on her water bill that was past due, was to take showers with her daughter and bathe quickly, therefore she got undressed and joined her disabled child. Even though Cynthia was terribly disappointed and angered that she could not be there during Grace's times of need, she was confident that everyone who had wronged them would pay dearly and thus disclosed her vengeful plans to her daughter. Once out of the shower, Cynthia gave Grace half the formula she got from Mama Devow as directed, before she assembled whatever else the witch requested. Before laying down with her daughter to put her to sleep Cynthia got her hammer and nails and reattached the boards across the window that the youths kicked in to gain entry.

The next morning felt like the day of redemption as Cynthia who slept comfortably opened her eyes and realized that she had spent the night with her daughter. The grieving mother wholeheartedly believed that since she met with the West Witch things had gone favorably well for her, therein she became quite eager for them to make additional progress. For the first time since she was forced to leave Grace alone and primarily unattended in their home for the work force, Cynthia felt confident that everything would work out and her daughter's issues would eventually get resolved. After kissing Grace goodbye and locking the door securely, Cynthia gave her neighbor the key while passing by as she hurried to get to the witch's home before going to work. Without extra funds for leisure activities and miscellaneous items Cynthia's legs were her only means of transportation, hence, despite the long distance to travel she simply threw her purse over her shoulder and started walking. To avoid becoming the main topic of gossipers throughout her small town, the cautious mother stopped outside the witch's property entrance and ensured that no one saw her enter the grounds.

The nervousness Cynthia felt walking along the long driveway the day before was a distant memory as she anxiously strolled along under the cool shade provided by overhanging tree limbs. Barbara who expected the young female was standing by the door entrance the moment she walked up and offered their guest a pleasant welcome before leading her to the room where Madam Devow awaited. Inside the room one of Mama Devow's servants who had his entire body covered with white clay had just finished securing a ram goat to a structure that prevented the animal from moving. After showing Cynthia into the room the maid and the servant left and closed the door behind them, at which Barbara went about her duties until she was summoned to show their guest out. Mama Devow instructed her patient to sit across from her at the reading table and demanded the items she requested the female bring. After Cynthia presented the items the Obeah woman slid her a vile containing some dark colored ointment along with precise instructions.

"I want you to rub some of this ointment inside Grace's vagina before you leave for work in the morning; and anybody touch her inappropriately over the next month you will know. If them penis penetrate her that Peepee go shrivel up like a prune within six hours of the act; and if them doing that oral nastiness them is cursed to get severe lap jaw for the rest of them life! There will be no reversal for anyone affected, for all prognosis are final and irreversible! Are these your wishes?"

"Yes Ma'am, those my wishes!"

Cynthia scooped up the vile containing the potent serum and placed it inside a small compartment inside her purse and sat back, while Mama Devow used the items she brought to fulfill her final request. The Obeah practitioner had a huge pot made of copper that was connected underneath the reading table, that was accessible by sliding aside the covering. There was a bit of clear fluid inside the pot that glistened like the sparkling glare off a lightbulb. The old woman instructed her client to place both her hands at a specific place on the table and ensured she did not remove them until directed. Once Cynthia placed both of her hands on the table Mama Devow ordered her "to close her eyes" then proceeded to commence with a prayer, during which the Nyabinghi Drums started sounding in the background.

"My lord and ruler of this world who resides in the most desolate places hear my prayer and grant my request," repeated the Obeah woman six times in an ancient African dialect during which the Nyabinghi Drums got louder and louder!?

There was an assortment of herbs and powders in containers built on the side of the metallic pot that Dion used to cast her devilish spells. The clear fluid inside the pot turned dark and started bubbling as if there was a huge fire underneath it. Once the correct consistency was reached Mama Devow threw a dagger then added different herds and ointments into the mixture. After the bubbles grew freakishly large where they simply popped like balloons, the obeah woman stopped adding ingredients and began chanting.

"I praise only thee my lord Lucifer!"

Eventually the dagger that Dion tossed into the pot floated up inside one of the bubbles and the West Witch reached in and grabbed it. Cynthia had fallen unconscious under Mama Devow's mind control, nevertheless she felt the energy inside the room. The Old Woman took the dagger and went over to the ram goat, fell to one knee then grabbed onto the animal's testicles and cut it off. With the goat's bloody reproductive organs at hand, Mama Devow returned to the reading table and wrapped Cynthia's ex-husband's hairs around the bloody testicles then tossed it into the pot.

"Through the sacrifice and blood of this ram I renounce the powers of Herbert Clark's penis! May he never experience another erection and may he start financially providing for Grace Clark and Cynthia Clark! Through the powers of my lord, through the powers of my lord, through the powers of my lord Lucifer, Amen!"

Once Madam Devow finished with the ceremony Cynthia regained consciousness and began looking around as if she was confused about her location. The sight of the dead ram goat and the bloodied Obeah woman helped to retrieve her memory, whereby she felt assured that the necessary spell had been cast.

"Your request is fulfilled! Bring mi fifty thousand Jamaican dollars in a month's time when Herbert start paying you what him owe! Then another fifty the following month after that," said Mama Devow.

"Yes Ma'am, I thank you dearly," answered Cynthia as the door opened with both servants!

***

Mr. Herbert Clark was at work when he felt a sharp cramp in his groin that forced him to race to the bathroom to conduct a proper assessment. The pain got so excruciating that Herbert had to leave work and rush to the emergency department, where doctors ran a number of tests which provided negative results. Herbert went home later that afternoon and told his girlfriend who was an incredibly beautiful and sexy female who always gave him the urge to engage in coitus everyday he returned home. The only break from sex the desirable young hottie got was during her monthly menstruation, when she typically experienced terrible cramps and still had to fight off her sex craved partner. That evening his normal erection didn't spur from the enticement he normally felt by just staring or brushing up against his girlfriend, but he excused it as nothing and believed the sensation would eventually return.

Quite often Herbert would attack his girlfriend for a quick sexual encounter before he left for work in the mornings, but his penis didn't even register a slight flinch the next day. Herbert began giving serious thought to his condition while driving to work and conducted several conversations throughout the day with some of his close male friends to find out if any of them ever encountered such an experience. None of the men Herbert spoke with could relate to his problem, but he received some comfort from those who assured him that "whatever his deficiency, Viagra, Cialis or any related products would offer a cure". Thoughts of his predicament brought his crippled daughter to mind, hence after calling his personal doctor to set up an appointment Herbert gave his ex-wife an unexpected phone call.

***

Two days later while Cynthia was at work the four youths who often broke into her house kicked in the boards that she nailed up at the window and went in on Grace. The physically challenged young lady was evaluated by doctors who diagnosed that she had the reasoning capabilities of a four years old, therefore to her the deplorable act of getting raped wasn't quite understood. Even though the crippled teenager was on her monthly menstruation the four youths took turns raping her, before they raided the kitchen for something to eat then left the way they entered. When Cynthia returned home that night, she was indeed saddened yet happy for the first time to find her daughter again naked on the floor, as she lifted Grace into her wheelchair and brought her to the shower. With the estranged relationship between her ex-husband and herself on the mend, Cynthia phoned Herbert and disclosed what had happened, at which he vowed to pay for the burglar bars necessary for their protection. That night her anxiety kept her from falling asleep as she watched the news footage with great interest, until the most dynamic news story she ever heard reported got televised.

There was a huge commotion at the Savanna La Mar Public General Hospital, when a television news crew arrived to report on Gregory Lewis age fifteen, Thomas Fry age sixteen, Calvin Rollins age fifteen and Dale Dawkins age fourteen, who all reported the strangest medical cases ever recorded in Jamaican history. All four teenagers went to the hospital after their penises shriveled up like raisins and they became concerned for their overall health. Regardless of their predicament none of the youths wanted to confess to doctors how it was that they sustained their injuries, nevertheless they were admitted and quarantined for medical examinations. Because no physician had ever seen such a medical phenomenon, the youths' cases had to be documented for further studies, while doctors tried to reverse their condition and create means for them to urinate. The youths' peculiar injuries puzzled the medical professionals at the hospital who had never before seen infections as such, therefore they informed the police who went in and further questioned the young men. Cynthia wrote down all the boys' names and whatever information the news reporters had to announce about them, before she rolled over and smiled to herself as she went to sleep.

The next morning, before the single mother left for work, two men came by to measure the openings for the installation of burglar bars and provided the estimate for the job to Mr. Clark. The pleasant feeling Cynthia awoke with continued throughout the day as detectives investigating her daughter's molestation case got the laboratory results from semen taken from the crippled girl. The main detective on the case telephoned Cynthia to advise her that "they would be taking into custody the four youths whose semen samples linked them to the crime; and the arrests may get televised because the perpetrators had previously been hospitalized". Cynthia was on the job at the Holiday Inn Hotel where she worked as a maid, therefore she turned on the television in the room she was tidying and watched the news coverage on the four teens reported to have raped an underage female. A news cameraman was allowed to video the arresting officers taking into custody the hospitalized youths, although they refrained from mentioning the victim's name because of the sensitive nature of the case. In all her excitement Cynthia unconsciously gloated to Madge Sinclair who was one of the maids she had confided in regarding Grace's predicament, to which they both jumped around and cheered the arrests. As soon as Madge left the jubilant Mother's company the backstabbing gossiper telephoned several of her friends and began swirling rumors of Cynthia's involvement with sorcery practitioners.

That night when Cynthia returned home from her nurse's aide course, she felt a spirit of relief just seeing Grace as she had left her, knowing that those who molested her would never again get the opportunity to do so. After she fed her daughter and cozied in for the night Cynthia got surprised by a visit from her ex-husband who came by to visit their daughter and drop off some money to help with her expenses. While Herbert genuinely went by to see his daughter, the rumors about the curse Cynthia placed on the youths who raped Grace had already circulated throughout the small town, thus he was somewhat curious to unearth if she had gotten that vindictive?

Even though Herbert had seen his personal doctor and was given medication to try counteracting his symptoms, the health professionals were puzzled by his sudden malfunction and had no viable explanation. Herbert knew that Cynthia loved drinking Red Stripe Beer and brought along a case of twelve as a peace offering. By the time they began consuming their second beer during which Herbert estimated Cynthia had become more reasonable, he began questioning and accusing her of "devil worship". The vengeful mother denied all the accusations and kicked Herbert out of her home, during which she implied that 'the rumors were probably started by Herbert's new girlfriend!' Instead of engaging in a senseless quarrel with his ex-wife, a perplexed Herbert who was already traumatized by his impotency simply apologized and left. By the next morning, the burglar bars installers were back to put in the new security features that would at least prevent anyone from breaking in through the windows and door.

Chapter 4

Constable Glen Thompkins left the Obeah woman's house a changed man and drove back to the market area which he had abstained from since the embarrassing altercation. Without a suitable partner to watch his back, Officer Thompkins retrieved his unit's assigned Remington 12 Gauge Shotgun Rifle from the trunk and ensured his sidearm was locked and ready to fire. The street officers were advised by their superiors 'to refrain from going into certain areas without adequate backup due to the escalating violence,' yet still the lone constable parked his cruiser at the mouth of the market and casually walked the busy vendors' strip. Glen had advised his lieutenant earlier that morning that he had a doctor's appointment and was ordered to report to the courthouse thereafter and pick up his partner who was subpoenaed to testify at a murder trial. Instead of picking up his partner Constable Thompkins who aspired to eradicate all the filth from his hometown went on a manhunt for the thugs who aimed their guns at him. While passing several vendors' stalls, Glen overheard the whispers and mockery from spectators who had witnessed his most demoralizing moment on earth, but the more chatter he heard was the irater he became.

The revenge-seeking constable stopped and bought a Jelly Coconut to quench his thirst under the hot Jamaican sun. While chopping away an opening for his customer to enjoy the delicious coconut nectar, the vendor spoke softly to avoid anyone else hearing him offer information. The coconut salesman told Glen that, "he feared for his cousin's life because she was unable to pay the local extortionists their weekly rate for two straight weeks." To avoid exposing his informant Glen spoke into the tough green coconut shell and asked the machete wheeling vendor, what time of the day the collectors typically arrived and without uttering a single word the cautious salesman simply indicated with his eyes. The look of fear was indeed evident on the vendor's face as Constable Glen looked in the direction pointed and saw Ferro with another thug talking to a middle-age woman.

Instead of moving directly to the point of interest, Officer Thompkins walked off in the opposite direction, which led the coconut vendor to speculate that, 'he had grown scared and therefore fled.' The constable disappeared into the crowd and circled through the maze of vendors before reappearing behind the stall where the saleswoman was being hassled by the two extortionists. As he watched the thugs in action through cracks between the wooden stall, Glen felt disgust at the treatment the female received in broad daylight with no one going to her aid, whereby he remorselessly aimed his rifle at Ferro through a small hole and blasted the antagonist in the chest. The vendor who was being draped by the shirt color and slapped around got blood splattered on her clothing and became so terrified that she dropped to the ground and held her head screaming "Lord Jesus!" Glen walked out from behind her stall with his rifle pointed at the second man's head while his finger caressing the trigger. Ferro's partner who was busy following orders to 'confiscate most of the vendor's sales items,' dropped the bag he was packing and started reaching for his weapon that was shoved into his waist.

"Is hard-working people's money you Scums like to thief! Pull out the gun out of you waist boy," instructed Constable Thompkins!

THE DEVIL'S CONCUBINE

The nervous extortionist who initially thought about drawing his firearm lifted his hands to surrender, but thought the officer wanted him to remove and toss his weapon, therefore he slowly reached for the gun and took it out.

"Drop the gun boy," was the last thing said by the revenge seeking officer, before he fatally shot the man in the chest. Constable Glen who was primarily out for blood, helped the scared vendor to her feet and compassionately hugged her to relieve her fears!

"Thank you, officer! Thank you! I wish them did have more people like you on the force," said the Vendor!

***

The National Internal Affairs Department that regulates the conduct of all police departments across the island was in New Kingston, and, after hearing about the market shooting, the Director decided to investigate if any procedures were broken. The shooting happened on a Tuesday, however, by the time the head of the Internal Affairs Department awarded the case to two of their agents the ensuing Thursday, Constable Thompkins had already killed five additional criminals. To ensure that Glen didn't kill anyone else before the agents arrived in Savanna La Mar and interviewed him, orders were sent to the District Police Captain for him to get assigned office duties.

Agents Meloney Banks and Jonathan James of the Internal Affairs Office were the first police conduct investigators ever sent to the parish of Westmoreland. Therefore, news travelled around the small town about the national interest being given to their police force, particularly one officer. While the legend of Constable Thompkins was slowly becoming a household story to the local citizens, his name had already grown infamous amongst the various criminal entities in Savanna La Mar to the extent they nicknamed him "Officer Executioner!" Within a few days, Glen had managed to develop a lengthy list of enemies from gangbangers to mobsters, and they all wished to kill him merely because none of their organizations were willing to surrender power of the streets to the proper authorities.

MAMA DEVOW

In an attempt to illustrate to the Internal Affairs agents and the local police squad that they were not to be intimidated, Ferro's crew of mobsters waited until they received word that the interview had begun then launched their plot to sabotage the proceedings. At 10:23 A.M., Bully and 11 of his gunmen friends rode their bikes to the main police station between Great George Street and Beckford Street, where they dismounted and withdrew a selection of high-powered weapons. Pedestrians walking along the streets who observed the helmet wearing gunmen prepared for their assault, started fleeing in all directions with uncertainty, as the men proceeded to open fire on the police station from the front and both sides of the building.

Just before the onslaught began, two constables exited the front door of the police station and saw some of the thugs getting into position, so they scurried back inside and dived on the floor while simultaneously yelling about the attack. Officers inside the structure were forced to find protection or dropped to the ground from the barrage of bullets, as the gunners emptied up to three magazines each at the police station, before they all mounted their bikes and sped away. Agent Banks and her partner Agent James who had just begun their interview with Constable Thompkins, cancelled all inquiries and sighted in their report that all the officer's shootings were justified. After personally experiencing the level of criminality against whom Savanna La Mar's constables contended, both agents commended Officer Thompkins for his diligent work and hurried to get the hell out of town.

Following the shooting, a huge commotion developed where police officers sat up a barrier around their headquarters to collect whatever evidence was available, as news reporters and crowds of spectators swarmed to see what had transpired. Inside the station, Glen and other officials watched the video footage caught on their security cameras to determine who the shooters were before they went outside to take a look at damage. At the sight of his precinct Constable Thompkins walked across the street to Frank's Lunch Cart where he ate regularly and bought himself a Jerk Chicken box lunch and stood there in the midst of the mayhem and ate.

Having already killed seven dangerous individuals gained Glen the trust of many business owners and other residents, hence they would offer him information in confidence rather than any other officer. While partaking of his food the proprietor told Glen that "he had seen several the bikes that transported some of the shooters over on Darling Street at a restaurant/night club called 'Paradise Lounge,' although he wasn't exactly sure to whom they belonged. The Constable also learned from another witness that "she believed the shooters were there after him because a number of them kept shouting profanity against his name."

The location given to Thompkins was already well known to the constable, who had been privately investigating Ferro's gang and knew that was one of their primary hangouts. Constable Thompkins' duties as a street officer prevented him from soliciting other means to acquire the information, he wanted on the extortion crew, which would physically molest and scare vendors with violence and their huge weapons then tax them for selling along the roadsides. Glen believed that the owner of the Paradise Lounge establishment, a Mr. Harold Hebner, was the boss behind the extortion gang, but he did not have the physical evidence to prove his theory. Vendors throughout different areas of the town were being subjected to paying huge percentages of their weekly earnings or suffer the consequences of either losing their merchandise or getting physically injured. There had been six murders of street vendors who were robbed of their belongings and money and with no indictments made or suspects mentioned, fear among all street sellers only increased. Concerns of what could happen, not only to them but also their family members, caused those being taken advantage of to remain silent and avoid informing the police. The public's trust in their local police department had steadily declined over the years, to the extent that many citizens deferred from reporting certain crimes with fears that nothing would get done; or worst, some dishonest officer would provide the information divulged to the very same people whom the informants warned about.

***

There were three of the shooters inside the restaurant who had their motorcycles parked behind the building. The Lone Wolf Officer who most of his peers refused to partner up with because of his ballistic policing methods, turned onto the property and drove to the back of the establishment where two other thugs were smoking cigarettes. As the squad car crept around to the rear parking lots, Glen made eye contact with one the smokers whose nerves were already on edge, so he grabbed for the Uzi strapped to his body and started plastering the police cruiser with bullets. Constable Thompkins was forced to sneak through the opposite door away from the shelling with the car still rolling, before he armed himself and returned fire at the assailants. The police cruiser rolled until it crashed into a customer's car with Glen moving alongside the vehicle for protection. The pinned down officer got on his radio and alerted his dispatcher that he had found some of the shooters involved in the precinct incident and was presently under fire! Within four minutes, officers had the entire building surrounded with all the perpetrators trapped inside, after the shooters that fired on Constable Thompkins foolishly ran back inside the structure. A standoff ensued and a negotiator had to be summoned to reason with the gunmen locked inside the facility, considering there were other customers present. Officers blocked off the entire area and surrounded the building to ensure that no one escaped.

When backup arrived, Glen was insistent on bombarding the building, because he believed that the owner of the establishment was the head of the gang that assaulted the precinct. The Senior Ranking Officers took charge of the situation and went through proper protocol to defuse the situation. Officers could see the armed gunmen inside both entrances to the venue and had no idea how many customers were inside, therefore, they waited until the gunners decided on the next move. Following a two-hours deliberation the five shooters unexpectedly surrendered and came out with their hands held high, to which officers rushed in and ended the conflict.

After the wanted men were taken into custody, Constable Thompkins, who had never met the Paradise Lounge's owner, entered the facility where Mr. Harold Hebner's five-and-three-year-old sons, his wife, their two employees and eight customers were all seated comfortably. The detectives were speaking with the business owner to get an idea of what happened inside the restaurant when Glen entered and watched the proceeding for a few minutes, before he walked over to Harold and dragged him by the shirt collar, lifted him off the ground and slammed him against a wall. Glen then withdrew and pointed his firearm directly at the man's forehead, which astonished everyone present.

"I know it is you who send those boys to shoot up the station. But mark my words, I go put a bullet through you skull when I get the evidence to prove you did it," Glen threatened!

"Constable what are you doing? You don't realize that this man has just gone through a terrible experience," said the ranking officer Sergeant Mullings!

Glen released the restaurant owner and stormed out with his weapon at hand. The detectives and other officers rushed in to console the business owner and apologized for Glen's actions, while the senior ranking officer followed the young constable outside.

"Constable Thompkins may I have a word? I would like to first thank you for a job well done today, but I believe you should take the rest of the day off and go cool off at home," said Sergeant Mullings!

"Sir I believe it will be more beneficial if I help with the interrogations. I think we can get some incriminating information or get lucky and have one of them wanna-be gangsters turn evidence against them boss Mr. Hebner," Glen stated.

"I don't want you jumping to any conclusions, the man is a successful businessman who is fairly wealthy. So think about finding the rest of these no good scums and leave Mr. Hebner alone," Lamented the senior officer.

"Look how them punks spray up the police station and my squad car, them young boys a murderer! It is obvious him is the boss, cause the only reason them surrender is because Hebner don't want him family hurt. I have no doubt that he is the one purchasing and arming these thugs and I go prove it," declared Glen!

"Go home constable, I don't want you back at work until tomorrow you understand," instructed the Sergeant!

***

MAMA DEVOW

The embarrassing defilement of the police department became a major topic at the local town council meeting, where the mayor and other council members came together and unanimously voted to assemble a special police squad to eradicate or bring to justice all gang members associated with crime. The task of assembling such a ruthless vigilante team was given to the police chief who would be the only commanding officer the unit answered to. To begin the process, the chief screened through their personnel for a suitable candidate to lead the team. Constable Glen Thompkins' disregard for his personal safety when it came to apprehending a suspect made him the obvious front runner to lead the unit, hence he got promoted to sergeant detective and was given command of the unassembled Vanquish Squad. A dispute over who else should get assigned to the unit broke out immediately between Glen and the Chief, when the newest Sergeant Detective refused to work with anyone presently on the Savanna La Mar police force, but instead with officers from other precincts across the island.

As leader of the team Glen was eventually granted the privilege to select the other members and opted to choose officers who were all on disciplinary suspensions from their precincts. The officers chosen were people whose careers Glen had followed and admired for their vigilante type policing. The five officers selected by Glen were Delroy Pierce from Portmore, Officer Markus Dwyer from Spanish Town, Officer Grantley Rogers from Negril, Officer Bob Barker from Ocho Rios and Officer Paul Tapes from Montego Bay.

The day prior to the arrival of his new team members, Glen, who had been having problems and could not sleep at nights because of terrifying visions, went to visit Madam Devow. The West Witch met with Glen inside her consultation room where she candidly spoke with him and offered solutions to handling both his nightmares and his violent visions.

"How have you been my child?"

"I can't sleep at nights Mama Devow; and during the days all I want to smell, and taste is death."

Mama Devow took Glen's right hand into hers and ran her finger along his palm.

"The demon within you exist only for such catastrophes. I can see

THE DEVIL'S CONCUBINE

that you don't smoke and you only a social drinker. But to coexist with this demon you have to calm your nerves by smoking a bit of ganja and drown your sorrows in the John Crow Batty White Rum! Am I understood," instructed the obeah practitioner?

"Yes Ma'am!"

Chapter 5

In order for Deloris Devow, who was Dion Devow's granddaughter, to escape from Jamaica when she did, she received help from several members of the Seventh Day Adventist Church, located in Black River. The Adventist worshipers snuck her off the island on a boat that sailed to Cuba, before she got on a plane to Ottawa International Airport in Canada. A job had been prearranged for Deloris who became employed as the nanny and live-in maid for an eleven-year-judge of the Gatineau Circuit Court and his wife, who had adopted five orphan children from overseas institutions. Mr. and Mrs. Kensington, who were also fellow Adventist worshippers, picked up Deloris from the airport and drove her to their home which was located in Aylmer, Quebec. It had been six years since Deloris fled the island of Jamaica, on which she abandoned her 12-year-old daughter and her late husband over fear for her life after becoming a member of the Adventist church.

THE DEVIL'S CONCUBINE

As a young lady growing up in Savanna La Mar, Deloris scored 92 percent on her National Common Entrance Examination and gained the privilege to attend Montego Bay High School in St. James. To avoid the long commute each day to and from school, Deloris, who came from a prominent family, got placed in a boarding house near school. During her free time off classes, Deloris would explore the city with friends and often questioned the locals on the streets about the city's history. Some of the people to whom she introduced herself became rather fearful or even ran away, horrified, as if she was someone to fear. Deloris, who was accustomed to being chauffeured and pampered by her parents, found the behavior of certain people peculiar, hence that initiated her passion to investigate her family's heritage. The young student first questioned her mother who was financially supported by the family estate and thus reluctant to disclose anything of importance. Darma Devow, her mother, only advised her to appreciate the glories of her surname, which provoked her even further to seek out more answers.

One day, at the conclusion of her history class, Deloris lingered behind to ask her Professor Elijah Erickson, if there were any historic significance to her surname from Jamaica's past, to which her teacher recited portions of what he called, "an old folk tale!" The story involved slaves and the diaspora of African Black Magic and sounded like a scene taken from a horror movie, therefore Professor Erickson told it in a rather humorous faction.

According to the professor, "a beautiful slave girl whose last name was Devow wanted so dearly to change her projected future and those of her offspring that she routinely prayed to the Devil and vowed allegiance to him. Lucifer acknowledged her prayers and noted she was extremely desirable and approached her with a crucial proposition, which she accepted, and thus became his concubine. The beautiful slave girl was impregnated by the devil and produced an infant who grew up to become Jamaica's first Obeah woman, while she received the freedom and riches she requested. The Caucasian couple that originated from England had two sons, one of whom turned insane after drinking a glass filled with magic concoction, while the other got killed when a horse went crazy and kicked him in the head."

The plantation owners' surname eluded the professor until the middle of his tale when he remembered and blurted out, "McCarthy that was the English family's name! The father went off in a drunken rage one night after his son died and claimed he was going to kill all his slaves, but on his way to the slaves' quarters he was confronted by the Devow girl and aimed at her but could not pull the trigger. The little girl had some sort of mind control over their white owners, therefore she forced the slave master to put the shotgun into his mouth and kill himself. Instead of reporting the crime the slave master's wife who was an alcoholic, sat back in her rocking chair with a glass of rum and instructed other slaves to bury her husband in an unmarked grave. Mrs. McCarthy then covered up the crime and handled the plantation's affairs and lied to their friends by having them believe her husband had returned to England to attend to some important family business. Even though Mrs. McCarthy acted as if she were in charge of the family estate, she became no more than a white face to deter questions from authorities, because the little girl controlled and commanded her like a puppet. Mrs. McCarthy survived her sons and husband, and when she died a lawyer presented a will that named the Devil's concubine as the plantation inheritor."

Elijah did not believe in Obeah or thought that there was any relevance to those who practiced the art, hence nowhere throughout his story did he give credit to the little girl's mysterious powers. Although the professor refuted knowing all the factual evidence about the tale, he gave Deloris some helpful tips on where she could probably uncover more information and that was in the town of Black River, Saint Elizabeth.

The passion Deloris exhibited towards uncovering the truth about her family's history got sidetracked a few weeks later when she met the youth who would eventually become her husband. Deloris was at the Overton Plaza Shopping Center located across from her school with a friend getting some female personal items when she met Steve Hanson, who was a student who attended Cornwall College in Montego Bay. The young city youth captivated the country girl with his personality and charm, so they began conversing regularly and eventually started dating. The pair became inseparable and Steve would often bring her to his college's home soccer games where they would be decked out from head to toe in red and yellow colors. A few years went by and on Deloris' 23rd birthday their drunken celebration went way overboard and resulted in her getting pregnant. The same day she discovered she was pregnant her father, who was at home in Savanna La Mar, suffered a fatal heart attack and died before they could transport him to the hospital.

Deloris permanently relocated to Montego Bay to appease her partner who refused to live in the country. The two lovers lived in the Rose Hall district in a comfortable townhouse that was being paid for by the Devow Estate. Deloris had spent time with Grandmother Devow at her spectacular home on two separate occasions as a child, but never did she observe any evidence that the old woman was a witch although she was restricted from going to certain areas of the house. Grandmother Devow would often see visitors privately even during family visits, hence Deloris was under the impression that the Old Woman was some sort of physician. A few months after she gave birth to Daliah her mother visited their townhouse and insisted they bring the baby to visit her grandmother, who had to bless the child and baptize her in their faith. Deloris was never told of any of the ceremonies her daughter underwent, which were customary procedures that every child born to the Devow clan experienced. By the time they reached Mama Devow's estate Deloris, who had kept her mother's company during the long drive, thought she was too tired and went to take a nap, when in fact her grandmother concocted a spell that made her weary. During her absence Mama Devow baptized the girl in their faith and checked her daughter to determine if she was to be her successor, but the baby failed the qualification test.

Even though Deloris stopped pursuing the truth about her family history once she met Steve Hanson she constantly dreamt and thought there was something she must uncover, but her biggest motivation to continue happened when her daughter was 11 years old. Daliah was at Steve's parents' house with her grandparents one day when she turned to her grandfather who had only recently received a clean bill of health from his doctor and said, "take care grandpa, I go rub Nana back for you when you gone!" Mr. Hanson Senior was quick to disagree and told the little girl that "he'll be around for many more years to come," but he died in his sleep that very night. On the way to their townhouse a few evenings after that, a mini-bus driver who had been driving recklessly switched lanes illegally and almost caused Deloris to crash her car to which Daliah who was seated in the rear seat yelled out, "tell him to slow down mummy or the big truck go crush his van!" While watching the 11:00 P.M. news Deloris was dumbstruck to note the report of a fatal crash that killed six, where the same exact minibus had gotten crushed by a dump truck. Without hesitation, Deloris made her way to the Black River district in Saint Elizabeth where she visited the Public Records Department for insights on where to find additional information about her family's past. The old woman who worked at the Public Records Office after hearing her request gave her the address to the local Seventh Day Adventist Church and advised her "to speak with a Miss Carmen Kirkpatrick."

Miss Kirkpatrick was an elderly church member who was intentionally blinded by the West Witch over her daughter, whom she had brought to visit the old witch doctor for help years ago. Her daughter was being possessed by a spirit force that would molest her at certain times of the day. After the failures of countless doctors and priests, Carmen followed the advice of a friend and brought the girl to see Madam Devow, who examined her and advised the mother that "she must forget about her child because the girl had been chosen to serve the demonic realm!" Miss Kirkpatrick thought the witch was being preposterous and threatened to report everything she witnessed to the police, to which Madam Devow blew a hand full of dust into her eyes that blinded her. With Carmen reacting frantically to her loss of vision the West Witch sarcastically advised her to 'go run and tell,' before having her helper evict the client from the premises.

Carmen told Deloris some significant facts about her family history and other important factors she never knew. Through Carmen, Deloris discovered that each Devow female is cursed to have only one daughter and that their husbands are generally preselected and ordained to die before they reached 50 years of age. The revelations about the West Witch and their family ties to Lucifer sickened Deloris, who had to take a partial break during the story, after hearing that 'their bloodline came from the sperm of the Devil.' Among all the information offered, Deloris could only find comfort in one aspect, and that was in hearing that the only chance she had to reverse her fate was by pledging her life to god and get baptized in the faith. When Deloris enquired about bringing her daughter, the blind woman informed her that "every soul had to make their individual decisions," therefore her daughter would have to make the choice to denounce Satan and accept the Almighty's teachings. Once Deloris returned to Montego Bay, she could not accept the luxuries from her previous life knowing where all the money came from to acquire them, hence she relocated her family to an impoverished single room house in Mount Carey and left everything behind. Deloris continued visiting the church in Black River to speak with the old woman and prayed for the redemption of her soul, however they knew that it was guaranteed that the witch would find out about her blasphemy therefore she had to flee the country. As difficult as it was to abandon her daughter and her husband, Deloris knew she would return to abduct her daughter, but she first had to save her soul.

***

The following evening, after Deloris got safely smuggled off the island, Carmen Kirkpatrick, whose house was closer to the Adventist Church than the preacher's, came out on her way to the midweek sermon with her Bible in one hand and her cane to guide her path in the other. Lucy Drummond, the church caretaker, was opening the windows and door and Mr. and Mrs. Smith were approximately 30 yards away from the church with their lingering daughter a few paces behind them. There was still an hour and three minutes before the program was scheduled to begin, but the night had started to descend therefore it was a little dark outside. Mr. Smith was the deacon for the church and often arrived before Pastor D. Johnson to help assemble the hall for their congregation. All three adults and the little girl reported the same sequence of events, wherein a fierce and muscular bull, whose body glowed fiery red with breaths of fire exerting through its nostrils and humongous sharp and pointy horns, could be seen in the distance digging its right hoof into the ground as it prepared to charge. The rare sight of such a magnificent and mystical creature brought fear to the hearts of all who saw it, so they scrambled for protection unsure of its intentions. Lucy Drummond yelled for the vision impaired Carmen Kirkpatrick to "move out the way" as the creature barreled towards them, but the old woman had no idea where to go or what to move away from!? The fire breathing bull charged directly at Miss Kirkpatrick and pierced its sharp horns into her frail skin while lifting her off the ground, before the beast hoisted her some 20 feet into the air, after which she fell on her head and broke her neck. Nobody moved to Miss Kirkpatrick's aide for nearly two minutes

MAMA DEVOW

after the creature left as they were unsure if the beast would return.

Chapter 6

Deloris Devow's Air Canada flight landed at the Norman Manley International Airport in Kingston, instead of Sangster International Airport in Montego Bay, which was closer to her destination. The flight landed at 3 P.M. but by the time Deloris cleared customs and collected her luggage it was nearly 5:30 P.M. The route from Montego Bay airport would have gotten them to Black River much faster, and also have taken them through Savanna La Mar, therefore preventing the West Witch from detecting her presence and foiling their plans, they took the longer journey home. Deloris got picked up at the airport by two church sisters and the pastor for the Adventist Church in Black River, who all played a small role in her previous escape. The religious siblings joked and commented on God's greatness, in addition to their spiritual growth over the years, but refrained from discussing the monumental task ahead of them. When they arrived in

Black River, Deloris felt the need for God's strength and went into the church to pray. The Canadian resident never forgot the help given to her by Carmen Kirkpatrick and thus included her in all her prayers, knowing that the raging bull was sent to assassinate Carmen for her involvement in assisting her escape. Everyone assumed that Deloris would have prayed for a short time, but she, in fact, spent most of the night pleading for the Lord's assistance in being able to succeed, before she fell asleep at the foot of the pulpit.

The next morning, Deloris partook of a customary Jamaican breakfast with her church siblings, then telephoned Daliah after Tyliq left for work and gave her a list of specific instructions to follow for them to safely make it to a doctor's office in Montego Bay. The first step in getting Daliah off the island required her passing a physical examination by a licensed physician. Following the doctor's visit, they would then have to acquire a police record from the local police department, and finally, her passport and traveling documents, should everything go in order. Before Deloris left with her companions from Black River, that morning the Adventist worshipers got in a circle and said a prayer in the hope that they do not encounter any problems. Deloris was fortunate enough to work for a Canadian judge who graciously got certain affairs prearranged to ensure that Daliah's case file was given priority authorization, and placed at the top of the Immigration Department's filing list. Instead of simply purchasing a returnable visitor's plane ticket for Daliah to travel to Canada, to prevent her from having to leave the country Deloris sought to get her migrated. The Landed Immigrant filing process for Daliah was started in Canada by her mother, who had, over the years, acquired her Canadian citizenship status. Deloris was also given an extended leave of absence from her job and told 'to only return with her daughter and grandchild,' by employers who treasured having her in their home and would do anything to help.

For the plan to work, the church members used three vehicles to confuse whoever would be following Daliah and her baby, then transport them from one section of the city to the next. Going outdoors had become a major challenge for the young mother, who had to get encouragement from Deloris before she was able to walk down to the taxi stand. On her way down the hill, Daliah passed her neighbor in her yard hanging the clothes she had just washed on her clothesline, and thought about her personal undone chores. The old woman quickly withdrew her cell phone from her pocket and made a call, in which she only said "she left" then hung up. The devastation she felt from the night of the intrusion caused her to become skeptical of certain vehicles, so she neglected to climb aboard several taxies before boarding a mini-bus she recognized. Initially, there wasn't any sign of the Nissan Sunny or its conductor, but as the mini-bus travelled along Anchovy Road, the car appeared from nowhere and started pursuing. Before Daliah observed that the Sunny had begun following them. a woman came on the mini-bus and stood in the isle and started staring at her in an intrusive manner. The lady kept her eyes on the young mother and her baby throughout the entire trip and exited the bus with them once they disembarked in the city.

Pastor D. Johnson, who drove to pick up Deloris from the airport, could not assist, but the ladies who accompanied the preacher, Sister Lindsey Hinds and Sister Diane Brown, drove two of the vehicles and the third was driven by the church deacon Brother Smith. Daliah's appointment was set for 10:00 A.M. at a private doctor's office located at the Blue Diamond Shopping Plaza in Ironshore, which was one of the only private facilities where Canadian resident status applicants could get all the relevant tests done immediately for a fee. To avoid raising any suspicions, Daliah was advised to take a regular taxi into town and get off at the Barnet Street Fire Department. After exiting the taxi, Daliah was instructed to walk through the Craft Market, which was a popular tourist stop where visitors to the island purchased souvenir items from wood carvings to traditional clothing. The female was told to walk at a fast pace through the market and exit at the opposite end on Market Street, where a vehicle would be waiting to drive her to another location. While scurrying through the market Daliah noticed that she was being followed by the female she suspected on the bus, therefore, in her haste to gain some separation, she started running. As she neared the assigned location Daliah saw the car she was told to look for, but as she climbed aboard, she spotted the Nissan Sunny a few cars length back in traffic. Once the car she leapt aboard drove off in the constant traffic Daliah looked back through the rear window and noticed the female getting into the Nissan.

"That lady who just go into that car is following us," Daliah informed the male driver!

"Don't worry bout them, we have some contingency plans to lose them," said the driver.

Deacon Smith drove off and joined the thick rush of traffic heading directly towards the town square. To ensure the Nissan would give pursuit, the deacon made an ill-advised left turn across two lanes of traffic onto Harbor Street, drove down to Embassy Place and made a right turn then continued around to St. James Street. The Nissan vehicle made the same turns and was only three cars behind when the deacon stopped at the red light at St. James Street. The deacon realized that the occupants of the Nissan were serious about following Daliah when he turned right on the red light and sped down to Union Street where he made another right into the lane, to which their pursuers climbed onto the sidewalk to get around the vehicles ahead of them and drove right through the red light. By the time the Nissan got to Union Street, the deacon had turned left onto Strand Street and stopped in the road, which was so narrow that it was impossible for any vehicle to get around. Daliah had exited the car then ran to Market Street with her belongings, where her third vehicle transfer awaited her. The deacon sat in his car with the engine shut off while he pretended, he had encountered some sort of car trouble, at which he ignored the horn honking and swearing from motorists seeking to pass. The occupants of the Nissan Sunny were the most angered as they got blocked in by other vehicles vying to pass through the lane.

The next vehicle was driven by Sister Lindsey Hinds, who carried Daliah up Queens Drive to a private resort where only reserved guests were allowed on the property. The female driver drove to the reservation building and pulled up beside a blue Honda Accord, aboard which Deloris and Sister Diane waited. Both mother and daughter hugged tightly and immediately started weeping on each other's shoulder once Daliah climbed into the car. The terrified mother and her daughter were then covered with a sheet while they laid flat on the rear seat, as they exited the resort and drove to the appointment.

Instead of entering the facility through the front entrance, arrangements were made for them to sneak Daliah and her child in through the rear door, to avoid having anyone who had done dealings with the West Witch seeing them. Although Daliah did not believe in black magic and was not quite assured that her recent experiences all tied into each other, she had personally witnessed some things that caused her concern. Deloris had previously refrained from telling her daughter certain historical facts about their family, but she promised to divulge all she knew when they were safely away from the island. Daliah had a number of tests done by a Doctor Chan and his assistant, including the drawing of blood samples for lab work while her mother held the baby. There was no necessity for Danielle to undergo any of the tests her mother underwent, because children of her age are automatically assessed the same status as their parents. Incredibly enough, while everyone else was unable to see the symbol carved on Danielle's chest, Deloris like her daughter could clearly visibly see the markings.

After they got through at the doctor's office, Daliah and her daughter were snuck back through the rear door under the cover of the white sheet and into their awaiting transport. The Ironshore Police Station was approximately two hundred yards down the road and they drove there to get the police record requested by the Immigration Office. The Desk Sergeant and other officers inside the stationhouse were surprised and curious to know why the mother and daughter had to be hidden while entering, but Daliah explained she was experiencing domestic issues at home. Within 10 minutes the information they sought was acquired and, as they went to leave the building, the sergeant stopped them and gave Daliah his personal card and advised her to, "call him the next time her boyfriend got overly aggressive!"

***

Three days later, Daliah received a phone call from the Immigration & Naturalization Office in Kingston, for her to personally come in and sign for the receipt of both her daughter's and her passports, visas, as well as the necessary documents to reside in Canada. Daliah and her daughter were being granted the Landed Immigrant Status to travel abroad with, which would thereby put them on the path to becoming citizens. To pry Daliah away from the watchful eyes of the West Witch's goons, Deloris had her church associates utilize the same tactic, however both the male and female assigned to watch her daughter were prepared the second time. To avoid traffic blockage the male pursuers rode a Range Triumph Motorbike that comfortably seated his partner plus himself. Both pursuers were four vehicles behind the first transfer, where Daliah exited the stopped vehicle and hopped into a second, nevertheless they managed to pass between the disrupted cars and regained pursuit. On their way to Overton Plaza travelling on Church Street between St. James Street and St. Claver Avenue, a police officer walked out into the street with his hands held high to stop the traffic, and enabled the driver of a Brinks Truck to exit a driveway. The vehicle carrying Daliah was the first being halted by the officer, thus, to gain some separation between the pursuers and themselves, Daliah stuck her head through the window and yelled to the officer, "if I don't get my baby to the hospital right now, she is going to die!" Instead of stopping them the officer allowed them to pass through and stopped everybody else. After their last transfer, the young mother and her baby were taken to the Sangster's International Airport, where they boarded a chartered flight to Kingston. Arrangements had been made for them to commute to and from the Immigration office, so they were back on the airplane ready to return to Montego Bay within an hour and a half.

When they arrived home that evening, Tyliq had already returned from work and was furious that she had not prepared supper or done anything around the house. Daliah had always known her boyfriend to be a calm and unfazed individual, therefore she speculated his attitude may have been caused by the Witch, who suspected foul play. The room was much filthier than when the girls left earlier and appeared as if Tyliq had been thoroughly searching for clues. To maintain the utmost secrecy, all the travelling documents obtained from the Immigration Office were kept by Deloris in Black River. Since Madam Devow's intrusion on the young couple, Daliah's intimacy levels had declined drastically, therefore the night before she departed, she pretended to be ill to avoid engaging in coitus. The Air Canada flight on which she, her mother and her daughter were scheduled to depart was set for the next morning and the anxious young mother couldn't wait to leave the country. The next morning, while Tyliq prepared for work, Daliah pretended as if she was still asleep and waited until he left before she got out of bed, packed a suitcase for her daughter and herself and left him a note indicating that she had moved away, although she refrained from mentioning exactly to where.

THE DEVIL'S CONCUBINE

The old woman next door who seemed to be always present every time Daliah left her house was building a wood fire to roast a breadfruit, while she smoked her morning cigarette in an unconventional manner, with the flame end inserted into her mouth. The departing mother who believed that everyone who stared at her intrusively was a part of her grandmother's network, despisingly looked at the inquisitive neighbor then continued to the bottom of the hill. There was a police squad car parked by the side of the road with two officers inside, hence Daliah climbed aboard and they drove away.

"I want to thank you so much for helping me get away from this nightmare of a country," Daliah declared!

"No problem at all Miss Devow, like I told you at the precinct, anytime you need rescuing from this boyfriend of yours I'll be more than happy to assist you! This is my partner, Constable John Peek, by the way," said the driver.

"Hello, nice to meet you and thanks for your help also," said the female who constantly kept looking back through the rear window!

"No problem at all ma'am," answered Constable Peek!

An Audi A4 travelling at high speed slowed down while approaching the cruiser to avoid getting ticketed for speeding. Seconds later, the Nissan Sunny, for which the female checked crept up behind the Audi and began following both cars. It took Daliah a few moments to properly identify the car, but once she did she immediately alerted both officers to the danger. Constable Peek advised their nervous passenger "not to worry because they would handle the matter once they determined the vehicle was definitely pursuing them". They drove along Anchovy Road and down the treacherous Long Hill to Bogue Road, which took them to Alice Eldemire Drive where they turned left and continued to Howard Cooke Highway. After such a lengthy drive the officers felt content, they were being pursued by the Nissan vehicle, so once they stopped at the traffic light at West Green Avenue and Howard Cooke Highway, Constable Peek jumped out and started managing the traffic regardless of the operating light. The cruiser alone was allowed to go through, and with the Nissan caught two cars behind, its occupants had no choice but to wait until the officer signaled them through.

MAMA DEVOW

Daliah and Danielle reached the airport without any further incidents and met with Deloris who was also excited to once again be leaving the island. The appreciative young lady hugged and thanked the constable for his assistance before he left to pick up his abandoned partner. The Church Deacon and the two sisters who helped them were there to see them off, so they exchanged quite an emotional farewell believing they might never again see each other. Even though they were at the airport and close to her dreams of fleeing the country being realized, Daliah still felt skeptical that they would leave until they boarded, and the plane started rolling away from the gate. The plane slowly passed by the different docking gates and stopped to allow a gas truck to drive by, when Daliah looked through her window and saw the West Witch standing beside a helicopter. A look of fright overcame the fragile female who grabbed onto her mother's hand while tightly securing her daughter against her stomach. Deloris noticed her startled daughter and looked through the window at her grandmother who had a vengeful look on her face, therefore she quickly dragged down the shutter.

"Don't worry honey! She will bother us no more," Deloris exclaimed, as the plane continued onto the main runway and eventually took to the skies!

Chapter 7

The West Witch very rarely got angry, but whenever she did, her entire staff knew what some unsuspecting soul had coming. As soon as she arrived at her estate the witch charged by her maid and went immediately to her spells chamber, where Mr. Riley was prepped and awaited her. Even though the witch was eager to punish those who aided her siblings and demonstrate why people should never interfere in her affairs, business was paramount, and her first appointment was an important client.

"I apologize for my tardiness Mr. Riley, but let's begin," Mama Devow said.

"No problem Mother Devow, you're giving me back a life, so I'd wait months for you if I had to," Mr. Riley stated.

MAMA DEVOW

The witch brought the wooden peg and placed it between her patient's teeth for him to bite down on. With the soothing sounds from the Nyabinghi Drums beating in the background, Mama Devow said her prayers and began rubbing the desired ointment over Mr. Riley's entire body. While the ointment soaked into the skin the old woman retrieved the preheated black stones from the furnace and ensured they were not too hot to put on her patient. The Obeah practitioner went through the same process where she passed her hands over her patient's body and only stopped where she sensed a quantity of cancer cells. With her patient drugged by the scent from the ointment, the witch applied the heated black stones over the area, then used her magical powers to forcefully expunge the melted toxins from the body. Mr. Riley bit tightly onto the peg as the black cancer mucus seeped slowly through his penis and down into the pan below the cot. By the time they were through Mr. Riley and the madam were perspiring as if they had run for miles and it took the patient a few minutes to gather himself before he was able to function on his own.

After Mr. Riley departed, Mama Devow would customarily rest until her next appointment, but that morning she had some unfinished business to attend to. She advised the servant who entered to remove the pig "to prepare her vision mirror", at which the white painted skin worker removed a 6 ft. covered object from a closet. The servant brought the object to a section of the room where Hebrew markings formed a circle then proceeded to remove the black sheet that covered it revealing a non-reflective mirror, before he departed with the animal. The witch sealed the door behind her helper then gathered the products she required and began her demonic ceremony.

"Boom, boom, boom, boom, boom, boom! Boom, boom, boom, boom, boom, boom," the Nyabinghi Drums sounded continuously!

"My father and ruler of this planet; hear my cry and appoint my request," repeated Mama Devow six times to the beat of the drums, before she drank a red potion from a glass tube and started chanting in foreign tongues! "Visions of my vision, reveal to me what it is that I seek!"

A purple light shined through the non-reflective mirror and filled the entire room, so anyone connected to her network who had seen her siblings that morning appeared to her. The first visual connection she made where she watched the events unfold with her client was through the eyes of the old woman who lived next to Daliah, who got a clear identification of Constable John Peek. The male occupant of the Nissan Sunny identifiably recognized Constable Ralph Fisher who he saw as they turned left off Bogue Road onto Alice Eldemire Drive. The last client who saw her siblings was a taxi driver who transported two customers to the airport and caught a good view of Sister Linsey Hinds, Deacon Smith, and Sister Diane Brown as they embraced and gave their farewells. After acquiring the information she required, Mama Devow said an appreciative silent prayer to her master during which the purple light extinguished.

With the guilty parties identified the West Witch turned her focus to revenge where her only dilemma became how to inflict her judgement. The first victims to suffer were Constable Peek and Constable Fisher who both lived kilometers away in the parish of St. James. Mama Devow went to a private closet and opened an antique chest that contained different types of dolls and selected two colored males, brought them over to the cot in the middle of the room and used a red marker to write the constables' initials on them. The Obeah woman then simultaneously held each doll aloft and shouted at them, "the fires of Hell will roast you" before she carried them over to the fireplace and laid them inside. The Nyabinghi drummer started fiercely beating the drums as the witch danced and pranced about the chamber like an African folk dancer, during which she retrieved a 5-ml bottle of Kerosene Oil, a box of matches and a torch. While parading about the room the madam lit the torch, filled her mouth with some of the fluid from the bottle and went by the fireplace, held the burning torch in front of her face and blew the liquid through the fire at the dolls. Huge flames shot at both dolls and burnt them to ashes while the witch continued dancing as if she reveled in what was to occur.

***

Constable John Peek and his partner Constable Ralph Fisher both felt a sense of accomplishment knowing they helped a female and her child escape from an unsubstantiated abusive relationship. The officers drove about their assigned sector in the Ironshore district ensuring there were no crimes in progress or regulations being broken, which was their basic daily routine. Before going for lunch at noon the patrolling officers drove to the service station at the corner of Morgan Road and Ironshore Main Road to purchase gas for their cruiser. While the service attendant filled the gas tank, both officers sat inside the car debating where to eat. A pedestrian smoking a cigarette passed ahead of the cruiser on her way into the station's convenience store. To prevent an unforeseen tragedy, Constable Fisher rolled down the window and called out to the female to extinguish the cigarette.

The driver of a Mac Truck coming down the hill on Morgan Road approaching the busy Ironshore Road intersection, suffered a mild heart-attack and ran the red light, narrowly missing two cars travelling in the westbound lane. With the speeding truck barreling towards a bus filled with passengers in the eastbound lane, the driver yanked the steering wheel left to avoid the collision and knocked off the bus's rear bumper. The truck got redirected and started heading directly for the service station, with the driver slumped over the steering wheel unconscious. By the time the service attendant noticed the out-of-control truck. She panicked due to its proximity and failed to provide a warning, but the officers inside their cruiser could see nearby pedestrians running away franticly. The gas server tried to move away from the developing accident without realizing she still had the gas pump in hand, and thereby splashed gasoline along the driver's side and inside the cruiser. Both constables got dowsed with the gasoline and became infused, therefore they immediately began voicing their displeasure. The Mac truck struck the left rear corner of the cruiser and smashed the car against the gas pump, between which the gas server got crushed and killed instantly, before the car rolled forward and struck the passing pedestrian. The service attendant died squirting gasoline across the station floor, while the female pedestrian was sent airborne and lost control of everything she had at hand. The cigarette the female was smoking went flying before it landed in a puddle of gasoline and sparked a huge fire.

The force of the impact sunk in the entire right side of the cruiser and knocked Constable Peek unconscious, thereby he simply laid motionless against the dash. After damaging the police cruiser, the Mac truck tipped over on the right side and slid to a stop some 20 feet away. Constable Fisher who, like his partner, was not wearing a seatbelt, banged his head against the steering wheel, which opened a huge gash across his forehead. The injured officer had no idea what happened to them or that they were still in eminent danger, as he grabbed for his partner and checked his pulse to ascertain if he was still alive. Behind the cruiser, the fire that started quickly spread to everything flammable and ignited a huge explosion at the pump, before it followed the gas trail that led to the police car. The fire ran directly up and into the car and engulfed everything within, scalding away skin and flesh before the fire department arrived some four minutes later and extinguished the flames.

***

Mama Devow saw the remainder of her clients that day and returned to finish casting her wrath later that night. The Obeah practitioner brought a male servant into the barn with her and had him remove his clothing then lay on the floor, while she collected the desired items required for the ceremony from her black pouch. Madam Devow gave the painted skin servant a magic potion to drink, which rendered him unconscious although his eyes remained wide open. The Witch lit a red candle and slowly dripped the hot wax around her servant, before leaving the burning candle by the man's feet. With the Nyabinghi Drums beating at a slow rhythm the West Witch said her prayers to her master, then stood over the servant's head and hummed like a Buddhist Monk. After humming for five minutes the old woman poured some golden powder from a jar into the palm of her left hand and sprinkled it all over her servant.

"I call upon thee to do my bidding, oh mighty and powerful Rolling Calf! Enter this vessel and transform him as your replica, then scour the night and trample the enemies I have marked!"

The servant began cringing and screaming as his muscles expanded and his body started changing. The man's hands grew and took the shape of a muscular bull's limbs and his head and body transformed into the Rolling Calf creature. After the beast formed it lay still for a moment while its humongous horns extended, and its skin texture changed, and became fiery like the sun. Once the transformation was completed the beast stood tall and was almost twice the height of the old woman. The Rolling Calf looked into Mama Devow's eyes and noted its targets, before it stormed through the door and eventually disappeared in the darkness.

***

The Black River Adventist Church choir members held their midweek choir practice that night so the three targets on Madam Devow's hit list were present. Sister Linsey Hinds' husband had been sick and bedridden for days, therefore, immediately after they finished practicing, she went home. The 63-year-old mother of four lived in their three-bedroom home on East Road with her spouse and youngest son, who both still relied on her heavily as if they were still children. Linsey stopped at the local neighborhood supplies shop and bought a loaf of bread and a liter of milk and continued her way home. Sister Hinds would typically sing her church hymns wherever she went, but on this night her joyful singing would cost her dearly.

The Rolling Calf sent by the West Witch came charging from behind a neighbor's house and tore away a section of the fence as it strutted onto East Road, where two friends walking along the street were the first people to see the creature. Both teenage boys took off running down the road and ran pass Sister Hinds while screaming at her "to get off the street!" The contented church member, who believed the teenagers were rather clowning around, neglected the warnings until she heard the screams of other observers. Sister Hinds looked behind her and saw the fiery beast charging towards her and knew the creature had been sent directly to kill her. Instead of trying to flee the Adventist worshiper who knew she was not physically able to escape, turned and faced the attacking beast as she loudly rebuked the creature in Jesus' name. The Rolling Calf lowered its horns as if approached Linsey and pierced them through her, before it hoisted her high into the air and continued as she crashed to the ground. Almost as quickly as the flaming bull appeared, the creature did its damage then hopped a fence and vanished, leaving Sister Hinds dead only a few gates from her house.

THE DEVIL'S CONCUBINE

***

Deacon Smith lived rather close to Sister Hinds on East Lane which was to the north. The deacon's wife sang in the church choir and attended the practice, but he arrived before they finished to accompany her home. Since that tragic evening where they witnessed the killing of Carmen Kirkpatrick, Mrs. Smith had been scared to travel home alone. Their daughter was in high school and had to study for her exams and was inside their house doing just that. The Deacon and his wife were among the last group of people to leave the church, however, after a delightful walk home, the couple got within twelve meters of their gate when they got confronted by the fire breathing Rolling Calf. There were three youths walking towards the spouses from up the street who were in closer proximity to the beast, which completely ignored them and focused its attention on the Smiths. Despite being ignored, the youths turned and raced in the direction from which they came as if they were being chased.

The beast emerged from the Smiths' back yard and stood blocking the pathway as if it was waiting for them to return home, at which it started digging its right hoof into the dirt as it prepared to charge at its preys. As tired as the Smiths were after walking a long distance from the church, they both took off running from where they came to get away from the beast. The wife and husband ran as fast as they possibly could, but the Rolling Calf only kept closing the distance between them. Mr. Smith thought that the best was primarily after him, therefore he turned away from his wife and jumped the fence into a neighbor's yard. The beast neglected his wife and smashed through the fence after him, as he raced to the back of the house and prepared to leap another fence. The Rolling Calf caught up to the deacon before he reached the fence and pierced its horns through his back, then hoisted him above its head and threw him over onto the next property. With its intended target deceased the creature vanished into the dark of night, and thus abandoned Mrs. Smith who was never the same after that dreadful event.

MAMA DEVOW
***

Sister Diane Brown stayed back to help Lucy Drummond clean up the hall and arrange everything for their upcoming service assembly. The church sister generally spent a few hours after meetings and practices to socialize, therefore it was often quite late when they left the premises. Lucy had gotten to know Deloris and was happy to know she had safely escaped from the island, but she also remembered what happened to Carmen Kirkpatrick and advised her religious sibling to "be cautious." Neither of them knew that two of their church members had already been killed as they closed the lights and exited the door of the church.

Sister Brown first stepped out the building and waited for Lucy to close the door while she stretched and breathed in the cool night's air. Diane relaxingly shut her eyes for four seconds and reopened them to the most terrifying image she had ever seen. The Rolling Calf was charging directly at the church members as if it had a radar lock on its target. Sister Diane Brown had a mille second with which to avoid the creature's detrimental strike, but her feet felt like they weighed a ton and were impossible to lift. Sister Lucy Drummond closed the door and spun around to an awfully unexpected death as the Rolling Calf's horns bore through Diane and proceeded to pierce through her. The beast deposited the bodies of both ladies at the base of the church door and took off into the night having fulfilled all its obligations.

Chapter 8

Madge Sinclair, the female co-worker in whom Cynthia confided began stirring up trouble for her. Miss Sinclair decided against working beside the malicious maid and plotted to get her fired. To begin her rebellion against Cynthia, Madge convinced their co-workers on the cleaning team to stop all dealings with her and start filing grievances against her. Soon thereafter Cynthia began realizing that she was receiving the cold shoulder treatment by everyone she normally spoke to, but she ignored their actions and continued her immaculate duties. Matters quickly escalated between Cynthia and her co-workers who lied and influenced the management team to start inciting her warnings for conduct violations.

Each day presented their individual challenges for Cynthia who fought to maintain her sanity and simply do her job in order to pay her bills and

MAMA DEVOW

take care of her daughter. One day she came to work and her co-workers were either sprinkling lemon or tossing powder at her whenever she went by. The following day they began either reciting Bible verses or some manner of rebuking phrase whenever they encountered her, which led even some tourists to question why they referred to her as such. Two days after the insults began, a room already cleaned by Cynthia was ransacked and found as such when the guests who rented it entered. By the time the alienated maid returned to work the following morning her boss advised her "they were terminating her services effective immediately and she should leave the grounds at once!"

Cynthia collected her belongings and shamelessly left the resort to the derogatory insults from several employees and went directly to Madam Devow's home, where the Obeah woman was with Mr. Riley her first client. Barbara allowed her to wait for the lady of the house inside her maid's quarters, where she watched her local morning programs while doing some of her daily chores. Mama Devow's primary helper noticed that she was incensed about something and could use a bit of pampering, hence she took time and made her breakfast with a warm soothing tea to relax her while she waited. Within half an hour the West Witch was through with her client and knew to herself that Cynthia was on the premises, therefore she had her maid show the female in.

The instant Barbara closed the door Cynthia dove into her impending predicament and told her spiritual advisor everything that transpired. Mama Devow took the matter of people mocking her craft or threatening her clients extremely serious, hence Cynthia's request for "absolute retribution" sweetened her ears. Before unleashing her fury, the witch demanded that Cynthia "speak the names of all those who have offended her," whereby she called the names of four individuals including one from management. The troubled female wanted her job back despite the recent encounters and also demanded a raise in pay in the process!

Madge Sinclair was the first person targeted by Mama Devow, who wanted to send a compelling message through her judgement. Cynthia had never seen her spiritual advisor consume alcohol, but for that specific operation Madam Devow filled a glass with Black Wine, then drank a portion and gave her the remainder. The West Witch retrieved four black dolls from a chest inside the closet and brought them to the table, where she placed them all before Cynthia with a red marker.

THE DEVIL'S CONCUBINE

"Write them initials on the chest of each Dolly then spit in them faces and lay them face down on the table," instructed the Obeah Woman!

While her client did as ordered Mama Devow clasped her hands, and closed her eyes, and started praying to her god while the Nyabinghi Drums slowly sounded. By the time she got through with her prayer Cynthia had finished the writing and consumption of the wine, which led her to begin moving rather wobbly on the chair. Madam Devow used a mystical spell to ignite the fire inside the fireplace and gathered some utensils and other desired equipment. Cynthia felt slightly intoxicated from the small amount of wine and moments later found herself staring into the empty glass. The Obeah Woman sat across from her client wearing face paint that made her resemble a skeleton, which startled Cynthia who could not recall watching her apply the paint. The Witch grabbed the doll with the initials M.S and started speaking to it in a foreign language, "Madge Sinclair, you will hear no evil nor will speak of evil" before she dipped her dagger into a jar with black ointment and stabbed into each ear, then jammed the blade into the doll's mouth. The doll was then placed in a small pine box and put on the floor to the left of the madam who turned her attention to another doll.

Madge Sinclair was indeed proud of her actions whereby she boasted about her exploits to everyone who would listen that day. Before leaving work, the maid servants obtained a bottle of Champaign from management and toasted to ridding themselves of the Obeah practicing employee. All four individuals named to Mama Devow were in attendance, whereby they danced and pranced around and congratulated each other for coming together on such a controversial topic. Even though the hotel employees knew that Cynthia was enduring through tough times, none of them cared about her wellbeing or that of her child. Madge went to bed at midnight and got a sound and restful sleep, woke up the next morning and was preparing to get ready for work when a co-worker phoned her. The backstabbing maid only noticed the incoming call because the device illuminated, yet pressed the caller button and placed the phone next to her ears and said "hello," but she could hear nothing through the receiver. The hotel employee again repeated "hello" before she looked on the view screen and noticed that the call was connected. Madge's youngest daughter walked into the room and although she could visually see the girl's mouth moving, there was nothing coming from the voice box. Believing there was something wrong with her daughter Madge started feeling the girl's forehead, face and throat, but as she spoke none of her words were being heard by her child. The little girl shrugged off her mother and ran to get the rest of her siblings screaming, to which they all returned to Madge's room and unearthed her symptoms.

***

Even though Cynthia was wobbly on the chair her eyes drew focused on the Witch Doctor, who had secretly telepathically connected herself to her client. Dion could visibly see the people whom Cynthia marked down, which allowed her to inflict her judgement on them. While scanning the lifestyle of the next advocate to violate her client, the Old Woman visualized the man's faults and criminal activities and deciphered a way to make him remorseful. Mama Devow snatched the next doll from the table and started talking to it like an actual person in an unrecognized language.

"Keith Robinson, I see you like to watch other folk's business! Well let's see how you like it when them start get up in your affairs!?"

The initials written on the next doll were K.R, which stood for Keith Robinson who was Cynthia's supervisor at work. Keith was a married Christian, whose wife could not bear children, therefore, he would volunteer to head the Bible study program at church in order to spend time with the little ones. While Keith was away at work that day, his wife needed a hammer and a nail to hang a picture and went into the garage to search for the items she wanted. As she looked through a cupboard where Keith kept his sporting equipment, such as golf clubs, fishing rods, soccer shoes etc. Mrs. Robinson came across a small box that was hidden beneath several items and suspiciously opened it. The instant she removed the cover she dropped the box to the ground in disgust, after seeing children's underwear with blood stains on them. The items from the box fell across the floor at which Mrs. Robinson noticed a DVD and an envelope with pictures amongst other things. As she reached to pick up the DVD and photos one item caught her eye, which was a child's bracelet with the name Dre engraved on it. The woman fell to her knees and cried inconsolably knowing who the bracelet belonged to, before she rose to her feet and went inside to the DVD Player and put the disc inside.

While waiting for whatever was on the disc to begin the wife looked at the pictures and was astonished to find pornographic images involving her husband and several minors. It took immense courage to watch a minute of the footage recorded on the DVD, which was incriminating factual evidence that showed her husband taking part in sexual relations with little boys. Two of the boys Keith fondled on the video were sold to him by their impoverished parents, which was more disturbing to his wife who wished she could bear children. After a few minutes of watching the filthy recording the traumatized wife used her cell phone and called the police, then sat back on her sofa and made a second call to her sister. Mrs. Robinson went numb as the telephone got answered and could not utter a single word as the receiver at the other end began enquiring, "If she was ok?"

After a long pause on the phone Mrs. Robinson said, "Stacy, I think I know who killed your son Dre."

***

The West Witch again looked through Cynthia's thoughts and took note of the third individual that harassed her client, who was a female maid named Cheryl Myers. While uncovering Cheryl's profile the witch discovered that the maid was being hypocritical, because she also visited a local palm reader on a weekly basis and personally knew the family to one of the youths who raped Grace. The initial idea to start with the dashing of the powder and sprinkling of lemon came from this inquisitive employee, who stood a chance to gain a permanent position with Cynthia's release. Mama Devow snatched the third doll from the table and spoke to it as she did the two before.

"Cheryl Myers, so you is a snake in the grass I see. Then bleed," said the Witch Doctor as she dipped her dagger back into the black ointment and ran the blade across the doll's lower stomach, then stabbed it directly in the left palm!

Cheryl Myers was the last person that Madge Sinclair spoke to that night before she went to bed. Both ladies had a lengthy chat over the phone about Cynthia, who they degraded and even critiqued her handicapped daughter as being slutty. Following their conversation, Cheryl went to bed and was awakened later that night with cramps to her lower stomach and a sharp pain in her left hand. An examination of her pelvic area revealed that she was bleeding, which she found strange after completing her menstruation three days before, however she ran to the bathroom and put in a pad. The single mother, who had two children, was a lifelong superstitious individual who wore a guard ring, which she removed to stretch and exercise the ligaments in her cramped left hands. Removing the ring instantly caused the pain to subside, but Cheryl believing all was healed, placed the ring back onto her finger whereby the pain instantly returned.

Developing such cramps that caused bleeding and having to remove her guard ring to stop the pain to her hand, influenced Cheryl to speculate that some sort of Black Magic was afoot. Instead of visiting the Emergency Department like regular sick people, the next morning the maid called in sick to work and went directly to see her Bush Doctor. The self-proclaimed Obeah practitioner operated out of his home and called himself The Great Ayatollah, and would advertised that "he was the most powerful witch doctor throughout the Caribbean." When Cheryl arrived at her spiritual advisor's place there was already two customers ahead of her, so she had to wait a short while before she got called in.

"Welcome Sister Cheryl, I didn't expect you today! Come in sit down, what can I do for you," asked the Bush Doctor!?

Cheryl took the ring from her purse the instant she sat down across from The Great Ayatollah and tossed it on the table.

"From last night I get this cramp in my stomach that make me start bleed and I just finished my period! Plus, I can't put on that ring or is pure pain in my left hand," explained Cheryl!

"Is what you a tell me say, some apprentice undermined The Great Ayatollah," grievously stated the Obeah worker?

The Ayatollah who wore a long dark blue gown with him hair wrapped

THE DEVIL'S CONCUBINE

with a piece of dark blue cloth, picked up the ring off the table and walked over to a cupboard where he collected five small tubes, each filled with a different color ointment. The Bush Doctor brought the tubes back to the table and placed the ring in the center of a soup bowl, then sprinkled some of the ointment from each tube onto the ring. With that done the Obeahman washed the ring and dried it with a rag, then passed it back to Cheryl. As soon as the female started putting on the ring the sharp pain reoccurred, thus she removed it and slid it back across the table.

"I'm not putting that back on, it's curse," Cheryl exclaimed!

Infuriated the Great Ayatollah picked up the ring and slid it onto his pinky finger, which caused him to experience an epiphany that made him to fall to his knees and bowed to the ground in repentance. With his client watching baffled, the Great Ayatollah got up and rushed to the closet, removed a short whip then tore off his clothing and started beating himself.

"Great Ayatollah, what are you doing," Cheryl enquired?

"Get out of my place Hussy and never return! Is you bring this torment to me life, get out," shouted The Great Ayatollah, to which the female grabbed her belongings and ran from the residence!

While leaving the premises, Cheryl overheard her Bush Doctor crying and pleading, "I beg your forgiveness my Lord!"

Realizing at that point that she had no other alternatives, the aching female hopped aboard a taxi and drove to the hospital for a medical checkup.

***

By the time Mama Devow got to the final doll her next appointment had arrived and patiently waited. The last antagonist that interfered with Cynthia was a female named Joanne Pickle, who, like Cheryl Myers, should have just minded her own business. The West Witch noticed that she had gone over the time allowed and grabbed the doll by the neck and said to it "you breathed your last breath Joanne Pickle", as she squeezed the puppet's neck. Madam Devow tightly squeezed the doll's neck and brought it over to the fireplace, where she then tossed it into the fire and watched it burn. Having completed all the requests made of her, the Witch Doctor advised Cynthia that "all had been handled, thus when she got appointed to her new position the fee was half her paycheck for the next year."

Joanne Pickle went to bed the night following their debacle at work, feeling confident that she made the right decision supporting those who wanted Cynthia gone. Unlike most West Indians who were somewhat religious, Joanne was an Atheist who also had no belief in the dark side. Amongst the coworkers who united against Cynthia, Joanne was the only person who truly regretted her actions, but the time for apologies had passed. While she slept that night, a spiritual entity attacked her and wrapped its hand around her neck and began strangling her. Joanne awoke from her dream and felt the clutching grab around her throat and fought to remove the grip, but the entity was too strong and thereby strangled her.

***

When the management team at the hotel found out about the misfortunes of their four employees, the Chief Operator of the company telephoned Cynthia personally the next morning and begged her to "come see him to discuss a promotion." Fearing that his name might be added to the terminated female's list, the Chief Operator sought to redeem himself before he suffered the same fate. Among all the celebrators from the day before who had some foul comment, none of them spoke idly or disrespected Cynthia from that point on, in fact they all lined up and apologized the moment she returned. Cynthia got appointed to the new supervisor's position and returned to work that same day, earning more money with more benefits for her child and herself.

Chapter 9

The Vanquish Squad within the period of a week became the only police unit that criminals revered throughout Westmoreland. The squad travelled in pairs and rode around in all sorts of vehicles from flashy unmarked cars to junky old vehicles ready for the scrap yard, which gave the impression they were not who they truly were. On their first day together the plain clothes officers, who dressed like common thugs at times, went for drinks at a local tavern where certain criminal elements often met for business. Between the squad members four out of the six men were avid supporters of witchcraft and wore their guard rings proudly, therefore a feeling of contentment was felt by the majority knowing the extent to which their peers would go to protect them. None of the bad boy cops were married except to their jobs, moreover Glen was the only one within the crew who did not have any children. Coincidentally while the officers drank at one end of the tavern four men came in and sat down at a table and began conducting their illegal affairs. The members of the Vanquish Squad were a bit preoccupied socializing and complementing each other on the dangerous encounters they had experienced to notice the exchange of an envelope for a backpack.

Glen went to the restroom and decided to pick up another round of liquor on his way back to their table. The squad commander was adjusting his pants as he exited the men's room, when his badge that was attached to his belt got noticed by two of the dealers. As he walked to the bar Glen made eye contact with one of the men and immediately thought they were behaving strangely, but he ignored them and went about his affairs. While waiting on the tavern operator to prepare the drinks Glen stood observing the five other customers and the interior décor, before an intriguing photograph of Bob Marley on the wall behind the dealers caught his attention. One of the dealers who saw the police badge was high on Ecstasy and nervously speculated that Glen moved to secure the front entrance to allow his associates the chance to surround them.

Without any warning, the dealer withdrew a Ruger 360 Handgun and fired three shots at the Squad Commander who was fortunate he had been looking in that direction. Glen dropped to the ground and withdrew his firearm as he crawled behind the bar counter and ordered the bartender to "Get down!" Customers began lowering their heads and hiding beneath tables as all the dealers withdrew their weapons, but only two of the men were concentrated on Glen.

"Him is a police officer," yelled the man that discharged the weapon!

All four dealers withdrew their weapons, but the two men who had no idea what was going on tried to escape from the situation by running towards the entrance. Instead of discharging his weapon above the counter, Glen knelt by the bar gate where he presented less of a target. As the two men made it to the door, the first shot the Squad Commander fired struck the leading runner in the ribs and pitched him over an unoccupied table, thereby forcing his partner to abandon their exiting plot. In retaliation the second fleeing dealer dived behind another table and returned fire at Glen, who developed a sense of excitement when it came to violent clashes.

The dealer who initially shot at Glen spun in his associates' direction and fired two shots at them, but, while his bullets missed wildly, the officers' returns struck him several times in the upper body. Watching his companion tumble to the floor with blood squirting from his chest shocked the armed man next to the first shooter, who panicked and tried to and dived through the window next to him. As the man leapt into the air, two of the intoxicated sharpshooting officers shot him in his back, which caused him to crash through and fall face down on the patio. The last surviving dealer who sought cover behind the table forgot that bullets could pierce through wooden furniture, and thus got killed by Glen who punctured several holes through the table.

***

Officer Thompkins went undercover on the eighth day following the group's assembly, for the sole purpose of uncovering information about the gunners who shot up the police station. Glen got information that the men involved were from the community of Russia and personally volunteered to search through one of the most dangerous neighborhoods in Savanna La Mar for clues on who the men were. To safely enter a neighborhood of Russia's caliber and maneuver around without getting killed Glen had to devise a plot that would fool everyone in the community, hence he chose to portray a mentally deranged individual who lived on the street and roamed around daily. In order to convince people that he was what Jamaicans considered a "Madman," Glen had to come to terms with the facts that he would have to do some unsanitary and despicable things. The Commander of the Vanquish Squad dressed in a filthy three-quarter length black pants and a shirt so dirty that the original color could not be distinguished. Several cuts were put into his clothing that exposed his naked bottom and other body parts. He also had to walk barefoot on the heated asphalt, considering that was the way such people lived. Black tar and foul-smelling hog grease was rubbed on his skin that made him smell like defecation, with his hair twined up like that of a starting dreadlocks and a knotted thick beard. Without any identification or communicative device and only a Ratchet Knife and a palm camera, Glen entered a world he had never lived, but he was confident he would acquire the information necessary.

MAMA DEVOW

Glen started walking the streets with some form of garbage at hand while talking to himself; and seldom did something erratic that made people assume he had mental issues. The foul stench that breathed from Glen forced pedestrians to cross the road or do whatever possible to get away from him, hence no one tried visually identifying him as they were too busy hastily trying to flee. The undercover officer would search through garbage for food and eat whatever he found in the presence of witnesses, who would later vouch that he was indeed a "psychotic individual." The day Glen infiltrated the community of Russia and started walking about, the little boys who would often terrorize the neighborhood stoned him with huge rocks, which forced him to run deeper into the community to escape. After ridding himself of the rude little rascals, Glen saw a neighborhood standpipe and went to get a drink of water. With the hot sun beating down on him the undercover detective then found shade beneath a huge Almond Tree and laid down and slept.

By the time Glen opened his eyes it was dark, and his provoking stench was working to perfection by keeping the locals and even stay dogs away. There was a shop up the street at which they would play music at night, wherein a few local Jerk Chicken pan sellers would gather to sell their products, hence the young ladies and gunners who controlled the neighborhood would often gather there. Officer Thompkins expected if not to uncover any new information, then to at least obtain something to eat, considering he was starving. With the setting of the sun most citizens retired to their homes and even though Glen was not from the neighborhood, he remembered days past when the streets would still be festive with people late into the evening. The times had changed so drastically that the police department feared sending constables to certain sectors of town, therefore the thugs who ran those zones only worried about rivals from other junctions.

When Glen reached up the road, he stuck to the side less busy and found himself a seat by the neighbor's gate across from the shop. The sweet smell of the Jerk Chicken on the wooden grill had the Detective's stomach growling for a taste, but he composed himself and thought about his objective. Moments later the sound from a convoy of motorbikes drowned out the music as 30 riders pulled up and blocked the road, which forced other vehicles coming to turn around and find an alternate route. The assertive behavior of the bikers, who callously exposed their automatic weapons gave the detective the belief that they were the shooters for whom he searched, so he started taking secret photographs. A female who Glen was paying absolutely no attention to, walked up and handed him a piece of Jerk Chicken with a slice of white bread wrapped in a piece of Foil Paper. Despite his frowzy stench and character impersonation, Officer Thompkins had to tell the female "thank you" for her generosity as he had grown accustomed to people avoiding him.

When the female returned across the road her male companion on whose bike she came, was not pleased that she gave away the food that he bought for her, therefore he angrily stared at Glen who smirked while consuming the meal. As the detective continued pretending that he had no interest in the gang's affairs, a Range Rover jeep pulled up and Mr. Harold Hebner the owner of the Paradise Lounge stepped out. Bully, who had his riding helmet resting on top of his head was the first person to greet the restaurant owner who behaved like a regular to the community. Glen could not believe his incredible luck as he watched the thugs respectfully acknowledge their boss, who purchased cases of Red Stripe Beer and liquor for everyone. The neighborhood thugs enjoyed the ambiance and each other's company while Harold discussed business with Bully and three others. Once everyone appeared relaxed under a few beers and alcohol shots, Glen got up and started talking to his imaginary friend as he walked across the street secretly taking pictures. The thug whose female friend brought Glen the food was one of the men talking to Harold who was leaned up against his vehicle.

"Where this psychotic idiot going," stated Harold, who looked straight at the officer who assaulted him but had no idea who he was?

"Hey! Where you think you going Wacko? Move from round here," said the gunner who threw his empty beer bottle at Glen!

Officer Thompkins' reaction to the bottle that shattered at his feet would have convinced any none-believer that he suffered from mental issues, after he completely ignored the broken glass and walked directly through it. The accumulation of dirt underneath his feet from walking around barefoot protected him, as he escaped without any cuts or splinters. The Detective nonchalantly walked over to the side of the bar and picked up two pieces of unfinished cigarettes and placed them behind his ears. Glen then continued chatting with his imaginary friend as if that was how he found out about the cigarette, before he turned in another direction and walked slowly down the street.

"Why you don't leave the madman alone," Harold joked?

"Trust me general, I don't want none of those people around me, cause you never know what they go do," declared the gunner!

The disguise selected by Officer Thompkins allowed him to perform illogical tasks that basic officers could not, therefore, he walked down to the tree where he slept earlier and climbed to a level from which he could clearly watch the gang members. Although he had managed to get a few pictures Glen knew that they would require more physical evidence to obtain arrest warrants and guilty verdicts in court, thus he remained vigilant knowing that the people he pursued were far too complacent in their community. An hour later Harold climbed into his Range Rover with a female companion, at which four riders, including Bully, mounted their bikes and followed him. The small convoy passed by the tree in which Glen hid at about 50 m.p.h. and turned down a one-lane-road that was rocky and unpaved, which prevented the detective from pursuing because he had no shoes on his feet. Glen did not suspect they were heading very far and believed that following them could prove beneficial, so he willed himself to attempt the difficult task of running on a trail littered with sharp stones and broken bottles. While descending from the tree the Detective noticed a fifth biker starting his engine, before the man rode off in the direction that his associates travelled.

Glen ran across in the shadows and went along the lane the bikers took, and hid in the bushes to the side of the trail with his Ratchet Knife at hand. Once the biker turned the corner and his headlights shun along the trail, the madman stepped out of the shadows and stood in the middle of the narrow pathway. To avoid striking Glen the rider swerved and escaped the collision, but, as he narrowly rode by Glen stabbed him directly in the neck. The rider crashed in the bushes, at which the officer ran over and recovered his knife, then searched the man and took his cell phone and a Glock 40 handgun. The Undercover Detective could still faintly hear the bikers' engines up ahead and estimated they were probably a mile away, as he hid his body in tall brushes and stole the bike.

The neighborhood thugs drove for nearly a mile before they reached a small house where four gunners guarded the premises. The house sitters were called out to transport three crates from Harold's trunk into the house, before they all returned inside to conclude their affairs. Glen rode up the trail and passed two small houses before he reached the broken-down hideout where Harold's jeep confirmed he was at the correct address. After hiding the stolen bike, the detective snuck close to a window and watched the men remove several A-K 47 Assault Rifles and various types of handguns from the crates. While his thugs familiarized themselves with their new toys, Harold brought his female companion in the next room where they engaged in coitus. Because Glen followed his instincts, he was able to capture on film the incriminating evidence he so desperately wanted, however he had to fight the urge to engage the thugs alone.

With Harold and his goons inside the house hiding their weapons in a trapped box built into the floor, the detective crept away to a remote area where he phoned his commander and discussed his findings. Prior to the actual phone call, Glen emailed his commander three pictures of the thugs handling the automatic weapons, which he knew would get a warrant approved without going through the proper channels. It was 1:08 A.M. when Glen finished speaking with his commander, who gave him the green light to execute whatever action he deemed necessary to bring the responsible criminals to justice. Immediately following their conversation, Officer Thompkins contacted his team members and arranged an early morning raid for 5:00 A.M. which was when he presumed the thugs would be tired and too intoxicated to mount a defense.

To enable the rest of the Vanquish Squad members to safely drive into Russia, Glen had to disrupt the local thugs' defensive capabilities, or his peers would end up getting slaughtered. The detective did not know exactly where around Russia all the weapons were stored, but he felt assured there was a substantial amount lingering throughout. Considering it was impossible to retrieve all the guns throughout the garrison, Glen decided to do the next best thing, which was to exterminate a few dangerous thugs and lessen their numbers. The decision on where to begin his assault was quite easy after having threatened Mr. Hebner "what he would do to him once he got the required evidence," but by the time he returned to the stash house Harold's jeep was already gone. Glen snuck a peek through a window and saw six men inside the house watching a movie on a small 22-inch television, while they drank Wray & Nephew

MAMA DEVOW
40% Overproof White Rum and smoked huge Marijuana joints.

    The Undercover Detective snuck away from the window and got a running start from approximately ten yards away, before he crashed through the wooden pane windows and caught everybody by surprise. Officer Executioner flipped once like a tumbler and sprung to his feet, then immediately began shooting from one side of the room to the next, whereby he killed everyone before anyone managed to get their hand on a weapon. After killing all the gunners, Glen walked over to one of the men seated on a sofa with a burning Marijuana joint on his lap and confiscated it, then took a deep drag and held the fumes in for a few seconds, before he slowly exhaled. While partaking of the joint, the detective fixed himself a stout drink of White Rum and chased it with water, then drank down the harsh liquid like it was juice. An inspection of the neighborhood thugs' armory stash frightened Glen, who had never before seen some of the hardware they possessed. Following his inspection, the detective armed himself with an A-K 47 Rifle that had a night scope mounted on top, two other handguns and additional magazines for each weapon. To safely carry both handguns Glen removed one of his victim's belt and used it to secure the firearms to his body, then went back out into the night.

    As far as Detective Thompkins' was concerned, everyone involved with the neighborhood gang was in some ways guilty, if not for shooting up his precinct, then for some other violation, hence he had no problem killing them all if necessary. After retrieving the motorbike, Glen rode back to where he killed the vehicle's owner and parked it in the bushes. Knowing that there was a high probability that his victims' associates overheard the shots and were on guard, the investigator resorted to his deceptive tactics that got him to the dance. With both handguns secured against his body underneath his shirt and the AK strapped behind his back, the madman slowly walked back up to the shop where many of the thugs were still drinking and enjoying the vibes. All the thugs were accustomed to their comrades freely exercising their arms from time to time, therefore none of them were concerned about the eruption of gunfire earlier. The troublemaker who chased away the detective before, saw the assumed mentally deranged individual coming up the street and looked to impress his friends at Glen's expense.

    "Why don't this mad boy go find some dirty gutter and go sleep," argued the Young Thug?

"Yow, leave the madman alone before him really get mad and do you something," joked an associate, which caused others to laugh!

The thug searched for and found a sizable rock on the ground and threw it at the approaching madman's head, but the stone missed and flew by Glen's right ear. Instead of retreating in the opposite direction as speculated, the detective surprised everyone and continued walking towards the mob. It was still dark and most of the gangsters were intoxicated with blurred visions and could not identify the rifle nozzle that stuck up behind the madman's shoulder. The witnesses present began laughing and teasing their brother at arms for missing his target, while some applauded the stubborn homeless individual for his tenacity.

The thug who threw the rock felt ashamed and started looking around for another, but Glen had decided against allowing the troublemaker another opportunity and thus flipped the rifle into the firing position. For a split second it appeared as if everyone believed the madman was illiterate to the handling of the weapon, until bullets started flying through the nozzle. The group of festive misfits dispersed immediately, during which Glen shot and killed five males, two females and injured three others in the commotion, before he was forced to find protection against the returned onslaught.

Russia's defenders although rattled, were far from submissive, hence they demonstrated their defiance and pinned Detective Thompkins behind a parked car. With bullets sailing overhead and crashing into his sole line of defense, Glen held his position against 19 shooters who were unable to advance. For the first few minutes, the under-sieged thugs simply hid wherever they found protection and fired their weapons in the madman's direction. To further infuriate his opponents and motivate their desire for revenge, the detective shot up several of their motorcycles and destroyed them. The three injured thugs on the ground were screaming in pain for medical attention, but Glen refused to offer the gang any relief and shot at whoever attempted to rescue them.

Three of the local thugs believed they could sneak behind the shop and three other houses and get close enough to shoot and kill their antagonist. The armed locals abandoned their group and snuck behind the shop and the first house, but a mongrel dog in the second yard barked at them and gave away their ambush scheme. Thompkins looked through his night scope from where the barking came and caught the second thug racing across a yard to a zinc fence, from which they planned to move to their strategic destination. Officer Executioner shot the man directly in the head then aimed at the zinc fence and fired three shots through it. The thug who was crouched behind the fence was almost shot and panicked, thus he got up and started running back from where they came. Glen shot and killed the man before he could escape, then pointed his weapon back at their posse and fired off a few more rounds. After seeing his two companions shot dead only yards away from him, the third ambusher turned back and returned to their original location.

At 4:58 A.M. the neighborhood nuisance received a call from one of the members of his Vanquish Squad team, who wanted his location and a safe pathway to get to him. Glen gave his comrade directions that brought them around behind him along a side street, from which it would be easier for them to rescue him. Detective Thompkins remarkably held off the gang of thugs until 5:07 A.M, when the remainder of his unit rode into Russia to extract him, seize the weapons discovered and possibly make some arrests. Without a bulletproof transport to protect them from the gunners' assault, the coppers parked a slight distance away from the gun battle and went in on foot for Glen. The gang members, who were waiting for daylight to forge an adequate attack, suddenly got bombarded as the extraction officers laid down cover fire to get their leader away.

Once they retrieved their commander and returned to their vehicle the officers drove directly to the weapons stash house to recover the illegal guns. Russia's gunners were simply not about to sit back and have anyone freely roam about their territory, therefore those who still had functioning bikes mounted up and started pursuing. The trail along which they rode was rocky and bumpy but the coppers' 4x4 transport was adequate for the journey. Glen's companions begged him to "sit in the rear carriage section" while they sat in the passenger seats, because he stunk far worse than when he left on the undercover assignment. With weapons spitting bullets through every widow including the sunroof, the six raiding officers made their way to the stash house located in the distant bushes. Glen, Delroy and Bob jumped out of their transport the instant they reached and formed a barricade that held their pursuers at bay while the other officers retrieved the weapons.

The three leading riders were shot off their bikes and their companions forced to dismount, hence they found protection behind trees and whatever else safeguarded them throughout the gun battle. During the difficult task of removing the crates of weapons, Officer Paul Tapes was shot in the left shoulder while leaving the premises, still they managed to remove all the guns from the house and loaded them into their 4X4 truck. After climbing back aboard their transport, the coppers realized that it would be suicide to attempt going back the way they came, so they continued along the trail which brought them into the adjoining Petersfield community.

The Vanquish Squad members dropped off Paul Tapes at the hospital to get stitched up and drove directly to Harold Hebner's house to arrest him. They arrived at the night club owner's residence to find the front door wide open and items thrown about as if they departed in haste. The officers missed Harold and his family by only a few minutes after gang members from Russia Community telephoned him and alerted him about what happened. After such a disruptive and violent morning, the squad members decided against returning to Russia to capture Mr. Hebner; and instead, brought their confiscated evidence to the station and allowed the tension to subside.

Chapter 10

The moment the plane from Jamaica touched down in Canada and rolled to the gate, a flock of black crows started circling the airport terminal. Deloris, her daughter, and grandchild got picked up at the airport by the Kensington's, who welcomed Daliah and Danielle with open arms. The couple drove to their home in Aylmer, where Daliah and Danielle got introduced to their children, after which they ate and relaxed for a few hours then brought the newcomers to their personal residence. Nobody took notice of the crows that had followed them from the airport and continued to do so as long as Danielle was on foreign soil. Deloris wanted Daliah to have the freedom to do whatever she wanted, so she rented and furnished an apartment for her only four miles away. None of the adults noticed the crows following overhead during the short trip, but Danielle, who was being held by her mother, kept pointing and smiling at the birds. Mrs. Kensington gave

THE DEVIL'S CONCUBINE

her nanny the next three days off and insisted that Deloris spent her daughter's first few nights with her in Canada and got more acquainted.

After putting Danielle to bed that night, Deloris got a bottle of white wine from the refrigerator and two glasses and sat down around the dining table drinking with Daliah. While the ladies spoke in the kitchen area one of the black crows that pitched on the Maple Leaf tree outside the bedroom window flew onto the window's ledge and stood there staring at Danielle as she slept. Deloris had promised her daughter that she would tell her the entire story about their family's history at the appropriate time and she felt confident that the time was right.

"Leaving you in Jamaica was the hardest thing I ever did, but if I loved myself enough to save my soul, I had no choice but to leave the island! Now the name of the old woman who marked Danielle is Dion Devow and she is said to be the most powerful witch in the entire West Indies," Deloris began!

"But why did she put that mark on my baby's chest, and what does it mean," Daliah asked?

"In order for me to tell you about her I have to start at the very beginning, where, on June the sixth, 1650, a female slave known as Dequalia Devow gave birth to a baby girl who was fathered by her white plantation master, Sir William McCarthy lll. It was considered an abomination for colored and white folks to reproduce, therefore, once Dequalia found out she was pregnant, she hid her pregnancy until a week before the due date then she revealed her predicament to Mrs. McCarthy. Dequalia made the decision to keep the baby because she wanted Mrs. McCarthy to know she was being molested sexually, and she hoped she would earn her freedom papers and get set free. Contrary to her belief Mrs. McCarthy behaved as if it was impossible for her husband to commit adultery with a slave and produce an albino baby, so her predicament only got worse instead," Deloris drank some wine from her glass.

"Dasheika Devow was a beautiful slave girl with light complexion and gorgeous hazel-colored eyes, yet still she experienced some of the worst forms of bigotry, where both races despised and scorned her. Dequalia was the house maid and did her best to protect her daughter, but she died when the little girl was four years old and the second maid named Idah Kizinguie raised Dasheika. The McCarthy couple had two sons,

MAMA DEVOW

Josh and Matthew, and lived in a seven-bedroom house that was on a 30 acres property where them grow cotton and sugar cane. Mrs. Catherine McCarthy suspected that her husband fathered the little girl because both of her sons had colic issues as babies and Dasheika experienced the same synthons. But stress over the years made Catherine start drinking heavily and, to relieve her anger, she would occasionally scold and punish the little girl."

"One night when Dasheika was 10 she went to refresh Catherine's glass of White Rum and tripped and broke the glass, so to punish her the enraged slave owner used a shattered piece of glass and cut her on the left cheek. Dasheika was rarely seen without a black eye or some sorts of cut or scratch to the face during her upbringing, but, through it all, her beauty still flourished. When Dasheika was 14 years old, William McCarthy caught both of his sons raping her in the shed behind their house. That occasion was the only time she felt it might be possible that her master could be her father, because William stopped them and advised his sons 'to never again put their penises in the vile sexual organ of a colored female!'"

"The hatred Dasheika felt towards nearly everyone she knew consumed her with vengeful thoughts, so she stopped worshiping God and started praying to Lucifer. Through her constant devotion, Satan keenly observed her immaculate beauty behind all the cuts and scars and developed a lust for Dasheika, therefore he orchestrated a plot where she and her future offspring would forever serve him. On the 31st of August 1665, Lucifer went to Dasheika in a dream and propositioned her with promises of freedom and wealth if she did his bidding. Dasheika, who would sell her soul to change her slavery predicament, agreed to the business transaction, following which, six days later, on the 6th of September, the devil again went to her while she slept on her cot, engaged in sexual relations and impregnated her. Then, precisely nine months later, on the 6th of June 1666, Dasheika who like her mother before her, banned her belly by using a cloth to wrap it tight and hold it compressed, gave birth to a fair complexion daughter named Doherty Devow."

"When the baby was born, Mr. McCarthy, who thought that one of his sons went against his warnings and created the abomination, took the baby and brought it to dispose of in a shallow grave somewhere on the plantation. Despite all of Dasheika's pleas, the slave owner brought the baby to a secluded area, dug a deep hole and was seconds from burying her alive. Some mystical energy empowered William to look into the child's eyes; and he turned right around and brought the baby straight back to her mother. Once her husband returned with the baby, Catherine McCarthy, who expected him to get rid of the child, took the little girl with evil intentions but only managed to bring her back unharmed. Like her husband before her, Catherine behaved far differently once she returned with the baby, as if they opted to become the child's adoptive parents instead. Unlike the other slaves who were beaten with whips and everything else, Doherty got nothing but love from the McCarthy's, who even gave her a furnished room to sleep in," Deloris again took a drink from her wine glass.

"Dasheika taught Doherty how and who to pray to in order to fulfill her arrangement with her master. Doherty who would eventually grow into a beautiful young girl was groomed with the malicious beliefs of her mother, added to the inhumane treatments she saw regularly on the plantation. One day when she was 11 she witnessed Matthew McCarthy strike her mother with an open hand across the face for answering inappropriately to a question. Contrary to his parents, Matthew never spent time or paid much attention to her, therefore he wasn't quite controlled by Doherty's hypnotizing powers. But as he walked by Doherty, she looked up at him and simply said, 'Mad!'"

"Later that night, she dreamt that she was walking in the cane fields and came across a red flower in a clearing. She picked the flower and brought it to the kitchen then crushed it and mixed the paste with lemon juice and gave it to Matthew to drink. The little girl envisioned every step she underwent and, the next day, everything unraveled just as she dreamt. One of her chores was to fetch refreshments for the slave owners and their guests, so later that evening when the McCarthy boys returned from tending to the fields, she gave Matthew the poisonous brew. Matthew drank the entire glass without a second thought and rushed off to clean up for supper. The potion worked instantly and struck him with a severe headache that forced him to skip dinner and go straight to bed. From that night on, only sleep could manage to bring a temporary relief to Matthew, because his migraines physically altered his ability to accomplish anything. The local doctor that they summoned was totally bewildered. After days of observation, he still couldn't figure out what was causing the headaches or develop a cure."

"Catherine made them board up all the windows in a room to make it dark and comfortable for her son to rest, but Matthew started having terrible nightmares where the graphic images were so realistic that he'd avoid sleeping, even though it was his only means to escape the throbbing migraines. His constant visions of turmoil and destruction made him become delusional, and, by the sixth day, Matthew was completely senile and ran away from the plantation. Hours after his disappearance, a plantation owner, miles away caught him having sex with his donkey, inside his barn, and brought Matthew back home. Something prevented him from going back into that house though, because he fought like crazy anybody who tried to make him go inside. The McCarthy's were forced to chain his ankle to a big tree in the back yard or risk losing him, and that's how Matthew lived out his life."

"All sorts of rumors started circulating about what caused Matthew's madness, but Idah the housemaid overheard a conversation between two elderly Africans who were certain that someone worked Voodoo and poisoned the young man. Once Idah told William what she heard the slave owner went crazy and grabbed his shotgun and went out to the slaves' quarters and said, "he was going to start killing niggers until someone told him who harmed his son". Then, with everyone pleading with him, he shot one of the men. As him select another buckshot in the shotgun, Doherty walked out into the yard and called out to William. In all his fury Mr. McCarthy spun around and aimed the weapon at the little girl but couldn't pull the trigger, so she made him place the gun beneath his chin and shoot off his head."

"Catherine, who was quite intoxicated in her rocking chair on the verandah, watched the entire thing unfold, then she calmly called out several of them slaves and had them bury Mr. McCarthy in some unmarked grave. The mother persuaded her other son Josh that his father committed suicide, but told everybody else that he had went back to England for a short time. Josh would die in an accident 15-years later and Catherine took care of that plantation for another 20 years before she passed away, and legally left the estate to Doherty in her will. By the time she died, Doherty was too powerful a witch for anyone to mess with, and she had every slave on the plantation hypnotized under her control. White folks were not really scared of black folks but they surely revered Madam Doherty Devow! So, Doherty became our family's first Obeah woman and throughout the years every few generations an heir is born to replace the current witch, and that is who Danielle is marked to become," Deloris explained!

After hearing such a repulsive story Daliah poured more wine into her glass quickly and chugged it down to calm her nerves then said, "So what do I have to do to change Danielle future?"

***

For three consecutive years Daliah and Deloris tried to get Danielle baptized at the church they attended, but each time a tragedy prevented the baptism from taking place. Although both ladies knew that nothing about salvation was guaranteed they themselves got baptized so as to denounce their family's curse. The first time they tried to get Danielle baptized was during the ceremony for two other church youngsters who both safely got anointed by holy water before the Jamaican born little girl was brought to the podium. It was a rather chilly autumn day, and the building was filled with worshipers some of whom only came to watch one of the three scheduled recipients get baptized. The flock of black crows that followed Danielle wherever she went were pitched on a pine tree outside the church and one specific bird sat on a window ledge watching the proceedings. All three Devow ladies were dressed in all white outfits like brides at their weddings, but they were especially more excited about the baptism than of anyone else getting anointed. Pastor Bruce Baxter, who would take the children from their parent then say a prayer before scooping up some water and pouring it on the top of the child's head, collected Danielle from Daliah and started praying. Once he finished blessing the child Pastor Baxter dipped his hand into the holy water which was at a soothing temperature only minutes before. The water was scolding hot and burnt the pastor who quickly retracted his hand and accidentally dropped Danielle into the baptism water as he grabbed his hand and crouched in pain. Daliah grabbed up her daughter from the holy water, which was back to the perfect temperature it was when the first two infants got baptized.

"What are you doing," screamed a frightened Daliah who looked at the pastor and noticed his injury?

Pastor Bruce Baxter received first degree burns after dipping his hand for a second, and thereby getting the skin melted off. The pastor's wife rushed to his aide with a towel and used it to carefully wrap the injured hand before they rushed him off to the hospital. Had not Daliah witnessed firsthand the pastor's decimated hand she might had gotten angry at him for dropping her child, but she was only left puzzled after retracting Danielle from the same water that caused his injury.

***

At the second baptism attempt eleven months later Pastor Baxter again presided over the ceremony and was very much looking forward to anointing Danielle after the first mishap. On that occasion, the pastor had two girls scheduled for baptism and, even though the second child was younger than Danielle, he chose to anoint her first. The ceremony began with Pastor Baxter welcoming everyone in attendance before he led off with a prayer. Following the prayer, the pastor had the choir sing a song from their hymn book before he went into commenting about 'the glories of God and the importance of getting baptized in the name of Jesus.'

The same issues occurred with the black crows wherever Danielle went, and thousands of miles away in Jamaica the West Witch watched the proceeding through the crows' visions. Madam Devow was locked inside her Reading Chamber and had the church ceremony featured on a huge screen along the wall, which was similar to having front row seats at the event. The West Witch had a white doll on the table ahead of her along with a small vile containing a minuscule amount of Mr. Riley's cancerous blood and a small needle. Dion spoke rapidly in another language as her eyes rolled back into her skull and froze showing only the sclera, to which she then picked up the pin, dipped it into the vile and stuck the doll directly in the heart. After she withdrew the pin her eyes continued the 360 degree turn backwards before the cornea reappeared.

Pastor Baxter had finished his baptism speech and asked the parents of the infants getting baptized to "please bring the babies forward." As Daliah proudly got up with Danielle and made the first step to the podium the pastor grabbed for his chest and crumbled to the ground kicking and shivering. A number of church sisters in the congregation screamed with fright and ran to their pastor's aide, where it was determined that he sustained a serious heart attack. The paramedics were called, and they transported Pastor Baxter to the hospital, hence church got cancelled for the day.

***

Pastor Baxter was still recovering from his heart attack a year after the incident happened and his congregation had a temporary replacement pastor named Ian Sutton. There were several rumors circulating around the Adventist church condemning the "Devilish child" as they referred to Danielle, for causing their beloved Pastor Baxter's injuries and Mrs. Baxter assured that she made the new preacher aware of their presumptions. Regardless of all the rumors told to Pastor Sutton, once Daliah and Deloris approached him to enquire if he could baptize Danielle he delightfully accepted. When Pastor Baxter's wife heard about the scheduled baptism, she drove directly to see Pastor Sutton and warned him against performing the ceremony, but the man of God courteously thanked her for visiting and disregarded her accusations. Throughout the history of baptisms performed at Pastor Baxter's Adventist Church the ceremonies have always included more than a single participant, but nobody wanted their child anointed on the same day as Danielle.

The night prior to the baptism an unidentified male riding a motorbike pulled up in front the church on Principale Street and looked around if anyone was watching, before he proceeded to remove two bottle torches from his backpack and used a lighter to spark the flints. To ensure that should anyone see him it would be difficult to identify him the rider kept his helmet on with the visor closed as he ran by two windows and threw the torches inside the building. Two separate balls of flames shot up inside the facility and the arsonist mounted his motorbike and rode away. Daliah had both her new white dress and Danielle's laid out on the bed waiting for their appointment in the morning when her mother

MAMA DEVOW

telephoned with the terrible news. The disappointed mother only broke into tears and hung up the phone, before she angrily took both dresses and tossed them into the garbage. Daliah went to lay beside and hug her daughter as she slept, and saw the black crow standing on the windowsill watching Danielle, so she chased the bird away and closed the curtains.

Chapter 11

The four youths who raped Grace Clark pled guilty to the criminal charges and were each mercifully sentenced to five years in prison among grown men. The female judge who presided over the case was somewhat lenient with the length of incarceration after discovering that the youths had sustained far more severe punishments for their crimes. After losing their genitals under mysterious circumstances, the rumors that they had been bewitched terrified the accused rapists, who all entered similar pleas with hopes that Cynthia would end her quest for vengeance? Neither Cynthia nor Grace had to attend any of the court proceedings as the lawyers withheld publicizing the victim's name due to the fact she was still a minor. However, on the day of sentencing, Cynthia was front and center inside the courtroom to personally hear the verdicts and ensure that the rapists who molested her daughter were headed for incarceration. Several audience members who came to support the youths shouted their displeasure at the judge while others broke out in tears as the security personnel remanded the youngsters into custody.

Inside the courthouse corridor, several relatives to the rapists who were sentenced confronted Cynthia as she departed and began shouting threatening and bias slurs at her. It was a well-known fact by then that she dealt with the most revered practitioner of Black Magic on the island, therefore regardless of their rants none of the hecklers dared to touch her. With her dark shades covering her eyes the unfazed victim's mother walked by the hecklers down the hallway and through the front door. Most of the hecklers followed Cynthia outside and continued pestering her in an attempt to expose her devilish deeds to others. Because the young rapists all pled guilty without a trial the court neglected mentioning much about the victim, hence their supporters believed Grace was probably some spoiled brat who cried rape to attract attention. To settle much of the disdain towards her Cynthia stopped and stepped to the hecklers and withdrew a photo of Grace in her wheelchair from her purse and showed it to them.

"This is the little girl that you bastard sons raped," Cynthia declared, before she continued on her way without any further disruptions!

Immediately after leaving the courthouse, the joyful mother telephoned Grace's father and gave him the thrilling news. Later that evening, Herbert went by his old house to celebrate with Cynthia and Grace, not having seen them since the night his ex-wife took exception to his comments. During the visit, Cynthia fixed Herbert a drink of which he took two sips and became drowsy before he fell asleep. Cynthia watched Herbert lustfully as he slept on the sofa, during which she noticed his wallet sticking out of his pocket and gently extracted it. With her ex-husband totally oblivious to what was going on she proceeded to look through the pictures and items stored. Cynthia abstained from interfering with Herbert's money and credit cards but found a picture of Paula, his girlfriend, behind one of Grace's photos and stole it from the wallet's contents. Herbert awoke at 2:12 A.M. and immediately checked the time on his watch, before he ensured all his belongings were accounted for and quietly snuck out of the house.

Cynthia Clark was determined to reclaim her deceitful husband and devised a plan to sabotage his relationship. Her trust in Mama Devow's abilities had led her to arrange a weekly scheduled visit during which she would get her palm read and future predicted. On her next visit to the witch doctor, Cynthia brought the picture and presented it to her spiritual advisor, with two requests for Dion to "fully disintegrate the relationship between the two" and "provide her a serum that would entice Herbert to return and never leave?"

"Do you still want him back knowing that the sensation in his penis will never return," Madam Devow asked?

"Yes Ma'am, I still love him and want him to come back home," Cynthia emphasized!

"Then tell me exactly what you want to happen to this gal," Dion questioned?

"I just want Herbert to realize she no good for him and to come back home," Cynthia stated.

"Since is so you want it, then so shall it be," The West Witch declared!

The Obeah practitioner walked over to the cabinet filled with her magical herbs, leaves and spices and took three bottles containing ointments, continued over to her doll chest and withdrew a stuffed puppet with a fitted box and returned to the table. With everything prepared, Madam Devow instructed Cynthia to 'close her eyes' in reverence as she first prayed to her master to bless the ceremony.

"To my lord Lucifer king of this world, I beg of thee to please listen and approve this request from your loyal earthly subject. In your name we have done wondrous works to increase your kingdom and shall continue to praise and worship you. I pray your rule endure till time indefinitely, and may every human grow to serve and recognize you as the only true god of this world!"

The flame on the candles around the room extinguished before they miraculously relit by themselves as the Nyabinghi Drums started beating in the background. Cynthia closed her eyes and placed both her hands on the table before she was instructed to by the witch, as she had become accustomed to Dion's routines through her numerous séance and spell casting sessions. To administer her spell, Mama Devow started chanting in her ancient African dialect as she rocked sideways then slowly faded into a trance.

When the Bush Doctor's eyes reopened minutes later, they had rolled back into her head and only the sclera could be seen, nevertheless she functioned normally and accomplished the necessary task proficiently. While Dion performed her devilish practice Cynthia's body got possessed by an entity that restricted her from opening her eyes or moving in any way. Madam Devow laid the doll on its back on the table and spread apart its legs, then opened two of the three serum bottles and tipped a drop of each ointment between the crotches. The witch proceeded to speak to the doll thereafter as if she was addressing a prostitute being sent out into the sex trade to intentionally solicit men.

"Miss Paula Dickson hear my every word and do my exact bidding! From this moment forth the toys that Herbert provided will cease to stimulate; and your lust for the sexual thrust of men will lead you to infidelity! May you become like the snake in the grass until you get catch, this I pray in the name of my lord. Hear my words, do my bidding, hear my words, do my bidding, hear my words, do my bidding! Amen!"

The West Witch could clearly envision Paula as she wrapped the picture around the doll and tied it with a red string, then placed the Puppet into the fitted box and again tied the box with another red string. With Cynthia still unable to move, Dion got up and took the box over to a section of the wall where small hidden compartments were built behind several bricks. The witch pulled out a specific brick from the bottom of the wall and placed the box into the hole and refitted the brick. To stabilize and seal the brick Madam Devow passed both her hands over the area and declared in her African dialect, "lock the grave!"

The Obeah Woman returned to the table where Cynthia was still unresponsive and sat down. The drummer beating the drums changed the cords of his beats to a much mellow tone which caused Dion to slowly lower her head onto her chest. After another minute, the drum was silenced, and the witch opened her eyes normally and raised her head. To revive Cynthia, Mama Devow simply snapped her fingers and her client jumped from her trance like a frightened child. Barbara the maid could be heard unlatching the locks to the door as if she was summoned telepathically by her mistress.

"Mix this fluid with some juice and give it to Herbert to drink and he will never look at another female," instructed Dion, who slid Cynthia the third bottle!

"Please tell me I go get my life back," Cynthia enquired?

"In due time my dear… In due time. See you next week my child," Mama Devow said!

***

Paula Dickson was at home that morning watching television in bed when she felt a cramp in her pelvic area and shoved her hand into her panty to check if she was getting her monthly menstruation. An inspection of her discharge revealed that she had sustained an orgasm even though she was not watching anything sexual or thinking as such. The sensation persisted where Paula developed the urge for the savagery treatment of a rough and intense male lover, thus she began fondling herself. It had been two years since she and Herbert engaged in sexual intercourse and she felt frustrated with having to rely on the satisfaction of manmade toys instead of her mate. With Herbert's impotent status a well-known fact, several local men had made advancements at Paula without his knowledge, hence she secretly kept phone numbers of people in whom she had an interest. After four years of devoted service, Paula telephoned one of the men whose number she had saved in her phone and thereby began a slew of promiscuous relationships.

Three Months Later

Herbert Clark returned home from work at an unusual hour one day with plans to take his girlfriend out to lunch and shopping. When he arrived at work that morning and telephoned his partner, Paula advised him that she had a headache and would be resting for a few hours, therefore, Herbert spent an hour and a half at the facility before returning home. After acquiring some roses to help brighten Paula's mood, Herbert drove home and carefully snuck into his house to avoid waking her. While removing his shoes at the front door he began hearing intimate moans coming from his bedroom, but he assumed his lady was stimulating herself with the sexual toys he bought her. With thoughts of joining his girlfriend in bed the impotent homeowner started unbuttoning his shirt as he made his way to the bedroom. As Herbert approached the door his girlfriend yelled out intimately, "Oh Tony, give it to me," to which he booted open the half-closed door and stormed inside.

There were clothes tossed about the room as if both intimate partners had ripped them off each other and a cell phone was set up on the dresser capturing the sex footage. At the sight of his girlfriend getting drilled in a compromising position, one of which he had never attempted, Herbert threw both his hands-on top of his head and lamented. "What the hell going on in here? Lord Jesus NO! You backstabbing bitch, I go kill you!"

The man with whom Paula committed infidelity shoved her aside and immediately started trying to negotiate. "Herbert please don't overreact, I'm only doing you a favor!"

"Favor, by sexing my gal when I at work!? I go get my machete and do you a favor, wait right there," Herbert argued, then stormed out to fetch the weapon!

"Honey, I'm sorry I didn't mean to! Oh God, him go kill us," cried Paula who ran from the room naked!

Once Paula's lover realized the severity of the threat, he also took off running naked from the room, where he cowardly pushed her out of his way as she exited through the front door. While scampering to escape unharmed the man sprained his right ankle as he jumped the fence, but the fear of getting killed compelled him to ignore the pain and he ran from the vicinity. By the time Herbert retrieved his machete and rushed outside to find the adulterers, his girlfriend was hysterically running down the street screaming, 'he is going to kill me,' but her sex partner was nowhere in sight.

Herbert was determined to get some sort of compensation and as he looked around to determine in which direction the male adulterer ran, he noticed the man's vehicle parked across the street. In his haste to escape

THE DEVIL'S CONCUBINE

the man abandoned all his belongings inside Herbert's house, including his car keys inside his pants pocket. To relieve some of his frustrations Herbert charged at the vehicle and started breaking the lights, puncturing all four tires, breaking the windows, and badly denting the frame. After succumbing to his emotions which caused temporarily insanity Herbert regained control and realized there were two youngsters across the street filming him on their cell phones. The embarrassed victim of adultery panicked and ran to his car before he sped off and drove directly to Cynthia's house, where he hid for a few days until the tension subsided.

Chapter 12

It had been four years since Harold Hebner evaded capture and moved into the community of Russia, where he was very well protected. The Paradise Lounge closed its doors the very day the owner went into exile, hence the police, in an attempt to locate Harold's whereabouts, placed his profile on the country's most wanted criminals list. Harold reopened another bar under an associate's name inside Russia's community, where the local gang increased their illegal tactics and closed the other liquor-providing establishments. Since the incident involving the Vanquish Squad transpired, the thugs took control of the manner in which the entire community operated and denied entry to visitors without an invitation, allowed fewer outside vehicles into the neighborhood and restricted police officers from entering their borders. Paramedics were the only emergency services allowed into the community, but even they were terrified to enter the garrison.

THE DEVIL'S CONCUBINE

The local thugs put in place several barricades constructed of rusted old appliances which blocked roads and redirected traffic through Russia; and would then shoot at anyone who interfered with their directional signals. The day that the thugs placed their disruptive items onto the roadway, a team of regular officers were sent to clear away the debris piled at the community's entrance. The officers sealed off the area and brought in a bulldozer to remove the constructed barricade, but, as the tractor approached the heap bullets began firing from a number of places inside Russia. The bulldozer operator leapt from the tractor and ran for his life, as even officers were forced to retreat from the area as the thugs shot at everybody and everything. Because of this every passenger transport, delivery services and non-resident who had no business in Russia stopped going there altogether.

To ensure the gunners were always prepared to defend against every sort of threat, the gangbangers fiercely carried and brandished their firearms around their community, even during broad daylight. Harold and his family relocated to a much smaller home with numerous armed guards to ward off any unexpected extradition teams sent by the government. Regardless of all the added security, for the first few years Harold secretly lived-in fear due to the knee-buckling warning given to him by Officer Executioner, in addition to the constant mentioning of the Vanquish Squad's accomplishments by news reporters over the airwaves. Nightmares where Harold envisioned Glen as a psychotic killer hunting for him prevented him from sleeping comfortably, therefore he would spend most nights at the bar around the thugs.

Wherever the gangbangers' main man went, he was constantly surrounded by four heavily armed thugs who allowed no one to get close without permission. Harold never left the confines of Russia and felt confident that no police or any other law enforcement agency were going to attempt risking the lives of their servicemen to capture him. With every developing year, Harold grew more and more confident he would remain a free citizen, as he continued importing firearms and used his colleagues to transact his illegal affairs.

The Vanquish Squad's leader received high praises from his peers and a medal for Exemplary Bravery for going into Russia and seizing the largest shipment of weapons ever found in the county. The most important gain Glen made while undercover was the trust of several residents in the community, who secretly began providing regular information on what was transpiring within the community's borders. The special unit assembled to eradicate gangs and illegal weapons discovered that most of the weapons sold in Westmoreland came from the community of Russia, which made it the primary hub for the guns being smuggled onto the streets. The Mayor and the police department were under immense pressure to close the pipeline for the weapons being shipped into Westmoreland permanently, regain control of the community and place Harold Hebner behind bars. However, the pundits were opposed to a full-scale war breaking out in public, where lunatic gunmen would intentionally murder unsuspecting police officers and pedestrians. As always, the most difficult tasks fell on the shoulders of the Vanquish Squad members, who were ordered to either extradite Harold or exterminate him.

Glen and his team chose December 31st to attempt the capture of Harold during the gang's annual end of year celebration party. The six team members started dressing in their black fatigues fitted with bulletproof vests around 8:00 P.M. that evening, after which they filled multiple magazine clips with bullets and ensured their knives, weapons and other apparels were intact. Each officer had his personal communication headsets, night vision goggles and two grenades should the situation become too intense. The confident group of trained officers joked around while smoking and drinking as if they intended on partying instead of working, which was their customary routine before heading out on raids. At 11:45 P.M. Glen received a phone call from one of his contacts inside Russia, after which they pulled black ski masks over their faces, mounted their SUV and rode out.

The Vanquish Squad members' rate of successful capture was 99.5%, but most criminals they brought in were in body bags. The person with whom Glen spoke before their departure was a 62-year- old resident named Lenny Famous who lived in Russia his entire life. Uncle Lenny, as he was most commonly known, was a lover of the White Rum and a pleasant, humored individual who always had a fiery remark for anything said to him. Mr. Famous used to drink at the old bar where the gang usually spent their late hours, and was there the night when they advised the owner that his establishment would be closing. The bar owner begged and protested but later that night gang members set fire to the structure and burnt it to the ground. Lenny was an electrician by trade and became a regular inside Harold's establishment from which he departed quite drunk each night, but over the period of his attendance he observed several acts of cruelty against which he took exception.

With everybody celebrating haughtily on the New Year's Eve Night, Uncle Lenny sat on his favorite bar stool drinking and surveying the establishment. The moment Harold arrived, the thugs in attendance loudly cheered his name as if he was their God. Lenny pretended that he was intoxicated and heading home and left the crowded bar, when he immediately telephoned Detective Thompkins and advised him that "their target was on site." For the arresting team to safely enter Russia unnoticed Lenny was asked to disrupt the young guards on duty or their plan would disintegrate before it got started.

There were several dark patches along the path, and the informant had to be at the entrance by 12:05 A.M, therefore, once Lenny got out of sight, he stopped pretending he was intoxicated and hurried. Once Uncle Lenny got within proximity of the guard station, he again started wobbling as if he was about to fall head over heels, as he started singing out loud which, was his typical behavior when drunk. The youths on guard were protected by a pileup of cars built behind the road blockage and could clearly see a large section of the roadway that ran past their territory. When the guards realized who was coming up the roadway behind them, they abandoned their station to have a little fun at Lenny's expense.

"Hey old man, you don't realize you pass your yard," shouted a guard as they began interfering with Lenny!

"Your mother have something old underneath her," argued a wobbly Lenny!

"Watch how you talk bout my mother," threatened the same individual!

"You prefer I talk about your batty boy father instead," said Lenny?

Two of the youths broke out with laughter over Lenny's lewd comments, to which their embarrassed companion charged at the Old Man and stomped him to the ground with a drop kick. The other guards realized their friend wasn't amused and rushed in to stop him before he

MAMA DEVOW

seriously injured or killed Lenny. None of the lookouts were aware they were being monitored by Glen and his associates who were positioned across the street, listening on Lenny's cellular which was left on inside his pocket. The invading officers used the deception and snuck into Russia unnoticed, then hid along the brushes and dark shadows to avoid being detected. The insulted guard was kicking Lenny on the ground when his companions rushed in and stopped him, so he walked away angry and returned to his assigned post. Both of the other youths helped Lenny to his feet, before they pointed him in the right direction and watched him stagger away.

Glen and his team waited until the guards had returned to their previously relaxed status and Uncle Lenny was safely away before they advanced from their positions. Each member of the anti-gang unit wanted to punish the youth who had beaten their Informant, but the success of their mission was pivotal to reclaiming the neighborhood. The overall mission was estimated to last several hours so to avoid any alarms getting sounded before they had Harold in handcuffs, they ignored the guards. The officers had acquired a detailed layout of the landscape around Harold's bar and mapped out a route to get there. While travelling along, Glen received a phone call from Lenny who wanted to inform them of his condition and offer his home as refuge should they require somewhere to flee. There was always a chance that their plans could backfire and, without much help behind enemy lines, Glen graciously accepted the offer.

The Vanquish Squad members separated into two groups and snuck behind houses into positions to the front and rear of the establishment. The bar was located at a T-Intersection with populated houses built around the structure. Due to the support from the neighbors who lived closest to the bar the officers were able to acquire lookout positions from which they surveyed the unruly thugs. Neighbors with guard dogs locked away their yard patrollers and allowed the officers to sneak into advantage areas from which they could operate successfully. There was a sound system playing music for the patrons in attendance, who were all drinking, smoking, and enjoying the ambiance. Many reports were made to the local police about the types and number of weapons being carried loosely around Russia, but the actual sight of youths partying the night away while heavily armed angered the officers. The raid team had received a report that Harold was inside the bar and planned on abducting him one way or the other, although they were not exactly sure how they were going to accomplish the task.

For the next five hours, the officers held their positions and watched the celebrating neighborhood disrupters' numbers dwindle as more and more of them got intoxicated and retired for the night. There was still well over 40 people present at 5 A.M. that morning when Glen decided they needed to make a move before the sun rose fully. Three male gunners left the New Year's celebration through the rear door and began staggeringly walking home along the rear path, but one of them stopped to urinate along the 4-foot-high fence that shielded Glen and his associates. None of the man's companions realized that he had stopped to pee and thus continued without waiting.

Officer Thompkins the Constant Illusionist thought of a plan and peeked through a hole in the zinc fence to ensure no one else was around. When Glen noticed the coast was clear, he crept behind the gunner and grabbed him by the neck and jammed his firearm against the man's temple. Before the frightened thug could raise his hands indicating surrender, Glen dragged him backwards into the yard and slammed him onto the ground. The man was stripped of all his clothes and handcuffed to a Plum Tree, as Glen changed into his attire and went back into the bar.

Detective Thompkins entered the establishment dressed in a Chicago Bulls fitted cap, a red T-shirt that matched the hat, black jeans, and a pair of Air Jordan sneakers. The DJ spinning the tunes was playing a set of soothing Lover's Rock type music for the partners present who were dancing rather intimately. Harold was standing in the corner to the left of the door with a beautiful chocolate complexion female draped all over him, without his regular security detail by his side. Everyone inside the venue acted as if Glen was no stranger to them and continued about their business, hence the detective felt comfortable maneuvering about although he kept his head slightly lowered and avoided actual eye contact with anyone. With all the freedom to exercise his warrant, Officer Executioner walked directly over to the occupied fugitive, grabbed the female by her weave and tossed her aside then jammed his firearm underneath the Wanted Man's chin. Detective Thompkins could see the fright in Harold's eyes as he ran his hand around his waist to make sure he wasn't armed, spun behind and grabbed him around the neck then pressed the weapon against his temple. The neighborhood gunners had by then noticed what was transpiring and formed a shooting squad across from Harold and Glen.

"What's your plan now hero? You think my dogs go just let you walk out of here alive with me," Harold threatened?

"My name is Officer Glen Thompkins, and I am arresting this man for multiple crimes. I would suggest you all stay out of police affairs or risk ending up like him," shouted Glen!

Glen slightly backed away his weapon from Harold's temple then unexpectedly thrust it at his captive, striking him along the hairline which opened a small gash. Harold jumped as if he had gotten shot and was obviously shaken to which Glen whispered in his left ear, "My orders is to execute you if I can't get out of here! Now tell your little girlfriends to lower them guns, and back up or we dying right here, right now!"

"Easy boys him not going anywhere, just lower the guns before one of you shoot me," Harold ordered!

Nearly everyone inside the bar slowly lowered their weapons except for Bully, who believed that there existed a personal conflict between the detective and himself. Bully stepped from the shadows across the bar where he also had a female whining on him, but opted to interfere with the situation instead. Once everyone started lowering their weapons Glen began dragging Harold towards the rear exit, when the unruly thug started walking towards them with his handgun pointed at both man's heads. Glen made sure he kept his head behind Harold's and offered the gunner nothing to shoot at in case he was an undisclosed sharpshooter.

"Take it easy Bully him can't get me out of Russia by himself, we deal with this outside," instructed Harold!

"Is long time I should have killed this idiot police boy," Bully declared as he wrinkled his face and slowly dropped his hand!

As soon as Bully's hand started descending Glen quickly shifted his aim away from his captive's head and hammered three shots into the community nuisance. The intruding officer shot and killed Bully with such speed and accuracy, that by the time Harold though about maneuvering to escape the weapon was back pointed at his temple. To reassure

THE DEVIL'S CONCUBINE

Harold that he would terminate him in an instant Glen burnt him with the hot gun nozzle and tightened his strangle hold around his neck. Everyone inside the bar was astonished to watch the officer murder arguably one of the most feared gunners in Russia, before he proceeded to continue dragging their leader from the establishment.

"V-Squad I'm coming out the back with the package, keep them lock down," Glen instructed his companions!

Seconds before the detective exited the bar with the man they had targeted, five shots rang out along the front of the bar as Harold's loyalists attempted to sneak around and lay await the arresting officer.

"What was that," Glen enquired?

"Just get some activists out the way, all clear," said one of the officer guarding the front of the bar!

Glen slowly backed out of the bar with Harold in a chokehold and his weapon pressed against the Wanted Man's head. There were people rushing to get inside the bar through the front door after they witnessed the killings of the ambushers sneaking around to the back of the building. The DJ had stopped playing the music as the entire atmosphere changed, hence those who were not gang members began seeking protective places to hide. None of the gangbangers had any idea how to rescue the man who funded their illegal operations and provided them arms, therefore the most notorious police officer in the parish walked away with his hostage. Officer Dwyer and the rest of the Vanquish Squad made sure that nobody exited the bar thereafter, by shooting at everyone who tampered with either doors. Harold was brought back behind the fence where he too was placed in handcuffs, as the sunlight from another day began brightening the skies.

With the mastermind behind the seizure of Russia detained, it became time to unveil the second phase of Law Enforcement's plot to liberate the residents of the community. Detective Thompkins telephoned their commander with an update and advised him of their success, to which he was ordered "to hold their position and not relinquish control until support arrived." Chief Kasey dispatched 110 police officers in tactical vehicles to shield them from possible snipers' bullets as they broke through the barricades used to segregate Russia. Each of the entrances that led into the community were bombarded by police officers who engaged in several shootouts with the few youths still sober enough to fight, however, each conflict was short lived as the more experienced officers took control of the neighborhood.

None of the officers camped outside the bar entrances were about to allow any of the gunners to leave the establishment, and fired warning shots at anyone who attempted. The officers' orders were to hold their position until reinforcements arrived, therefore they kept the task manageable by holding much of the gunners inside the bar hostage. Once the defenses had been breached and the officers stormed into the community, they still had to deal with the armed gangbangers inside the bar. To avoid a horrible massacre, Glen reasoned with Herbert and asked him to get his people to surrender or they would all be killed. Harold was front and center when Officer Thompkins mercilessly executed Bully and observed the lack of emotion the detective showed as he pulled the trigger, therefore, to avoid his associates being slaughtered he convinced his young gunners to surrender.

With the remaining gangbangers inside the community still intoxicated and asleep, the officers combed through the neighborhood and went door to door in a massive search for other members and their illegal weapons. At the end of their unsanctioned raids, the police tallied 119 arrests, 96 weapons seized, and eleven criminals killed. The honest, hard working people of Russia, who had lived under oppression for years, came out of their houses like survivors after a war ended and sincerely thanked the rescuing officers for saving them.

Chapter 13

Danielle grew up without many friends at school and became popularly known as "Black Bird" on account of the pesky crows that followed her wherever she went. The Kensington's treated the little girl like family, so she would play around inside their huge house for hours while her grandmother babysat and Daliah attended school. Even though the Kensington's lived a short distance away from Danielle she got included in all the family's events such as birthdays, vacations, and Christmases. Daliah wanted to become a Social Aide Worker but did not complete the necessary studies for the position during her time in Jamaica. To acquire the desired degree for the position, Daliah attended the University of Outaouais which was located only 15 miles away from her home.

People around the community never dismissed the incidents that transpired when Danielle was yet a little girl, and secretly blamed her for several other unexplainable phenomena that transpired during her upbringing. When Danielle was in the second grade, a little girl name Mano Beauvoin started bullying her by calling her names and physically hitting her. On a number of occasions their teacher, Mrs. Riviere, observed the mistreatment and instead of putting a stop to the abuse she allowed the injustice to continue. During art class one day, Danielle drew a photo of a man walking alongside a little girl holding hands. When asked by her teacher if the people on the picture were her father and her, Danielle explained that "the girl was Mano, and she was being led away by a strange blond-haired man who molested her then killed her!" The teacher thought that Danielle was attempting to retaliate for the abuse afflicted onto her by suggesting such a hideous crime, therefore she punished her by putting her on time out in the corner for the entire day.

Three days later, Mano got off her school bus in front of her gate and started walking towards the house that was 50 yards away. The family lived on a 10-acre property along the countryside where they saw deer and other wildlife creatures regularly. Mano's mother, Francine, who would customarily wait for her at the bus stop, decided that she was responsible enough to walk up on her own and watched her as she started up the driveway, before she turned away and went back to what she was doing previously. A family relative who Mano recognized and trusted pulled up in his Chevy Silverado and called to her from the entrance, so instead of continuing on her way she turned back and ran to him. "Uncle Teddy" as referred to by Mano, tricked her into believing he was going to pick her father up at work and return, therefore, intriguingly she asked to trot along?

By the time Mano's mother realized she did not walk into the house as expected, more than five minutes had elapsed, and her daughter was already almost 10 kilometers away. Mano's mother went outside and started calling for her, believing that she may have run around to the rear of the house to play. After shouting her daughter's name several times and checking everywhere she thought Mano could have gone, Francine became frantic once she realized that her child was indeed missing. The police were called in, and an immediate investigation was started where they sent out images of the little girl to every patrol unit around the area. Without any solid leads to work, with the police focused their initial

THE DEVIL'S CONCUBINE

search on the wooded areas around the family's house, but found nothing to suggest where the little girl could have possibly gone.

As the Silverado truck drove onto Highway-148, Mano realized they were driving away from her father's workplace and started fussing. While the little girl complained about wanting to return home, Teddy noticed a police cruiser approaching in his rear-view mirror. The child abductor panicked and struck Mano with a solid right punch that knocked her unconscious. Uncle Teddy drove his niece far away from home into the hills of Breckenridge, where he was quite familiar with the landscape. The family molester drove his Silverado into the woods and parked where it was impossible to see his vehicle, before he checked around to ensure the coast was clear then took Mano out of the truck. Teddy brought his niece to an area where his father used to bring him to hunt for deer as a child, where he ripped off her clothes and forcibly penetrated her. During coitus Mano awoke and started tussling and crying, to which Teddy placed his right hand over her mouth and held her securely with his left. Regardless of the fearful tears flowing from his niece's eyes, Teddy ravaged the little girl until he ejaculated and released his immobilizing grip. With Teddy cleaning himself, Mano got up and started running naked through the bushes in an attempt to get away from her pedophile uncle.

The child abductor could not afford to have the little girl miraculously find help or escape and alert law enforcement, therefore he took after her and chased her through the bushes. Mano gave her pursuing uncle an eventful chase, as she screamed at the top of her lungs "for help" while running. Despite all her efforts to escape, Teddy caught Mano by diving at her and dragging her to the ground by one leg, however she fought by kicking and tussling until he irritably picked up a boulder, and clobbered her on the side of the skull. Teddy wanted only to silence Mano, but struck her with such brute force, that he cracked her skull, and killed her instantly. With Mano lying motionless and silent, Teddy noticed the blood and dropped the rock from his hand, before he rose to his feet, looked around and ran from the scene.

Mano's body was discovered two-and-a-half months later, when a hiker and his dog came upon a foul stench that they trailed back to her naked corpse. The hiker became so perturbed by the sight of the child's body that he quickly moved away with his dog and phoned the police. Once the forensic team arrived, a more adequate radius of the crime scene was determined after they found Mano's clothes where Teddy molested her. The entire area got blocked off by investigators who searched intently for clues to help them solve the murder. Mano's clothing, the boulder used to strike her, and several other items were sent to the RCMP Forensic Lab for testing, as officers also contacted Francine and asked her "if she could identify her daughter's body at the hospital morgue?"

Rebecca Riviere the 2nd Grade teacher was getting ready for bed one night three weeks later when the news anchor reported a dramatic and surprising resolution in the case of her deceased student, Mano Beauvoin! RCMP Officers went to the home of a Mr. Theodore LaRoach who was a tall and stout, blond- hair Caucasian bachelor and arrested him for the rape and brutal murder of his niece. Rebecca's mouth dropped wide open as she watched the officers handle the murderer and thought about Danielle's comment and how she unfairly punished the little girl for what she said. The accurate depiction of such a hideous crime by a young student was somewhat unnerving, thus Rebecca cautiously changed the manner in which she dealt with Danielle from that moment forward.

***

Danielle was always capable of predicting people's future and diagnosing illnesses in humans who had no prior awareness of their sickness, but the older she grew, the more powerful she became. The body of the heir to the Devow family curse transformed differently from regular females, which caused her to appear far older than her actual age. Danielle regularly saw disembodied spirits that would possess and drive certain individuals insane and even spoke with spirit medians, which led people to believe she was mentally deranged. When she was nine years old, she hugged Mrs. Kensington inside the kitchen one day and her head brushed up against the woman's breast. The little girl somewhat startled Mrs. Kensington thereafter by placing her hand on her left breast for three seconds before removing it. Deloris, who was also inside the kitchen, rushed over and grabbed her granddaughter and advised her to apologize. Instead of apologizing to the lady, Danielle looked up at her with tears in her eye and said, "You have a cancer lump in your breast!"

THE DEVIL'S CONCUBINE

Even though Mrs. Kensington knew the little girl was not a registered physician she believed every word due to Danielle's track record and stumbled against the counter as she reached for the phone. The disheartened female telephoned her doctor's office and made an emergency appointment, following which she gracefully exited the kitchen and went to her bedroom and locked the door.

The following day Mrs. Kensington went to her appointment and had her doctor physically examine her, perform a Mammogram test, and collect blood samples for the laboratory examination. Even though her adopted children were well into their teenage and adult stages by then, Mrs. Kensington was terribly worried her life would be cut short by the disease. Following a lengthy discussion with her family physician, where he disclosed the most effective methods of treatment on the market and the leading institutions and doctors in the field her, fears of defeating the disease decreased. The Doctor advised her that "should the lump he detected be cancerous, because they discovered it at such an early stage, she had the best odds of beating the disease." The encouragement from her doctor gave Mrs. Kensington the confidence that, regardless the results, she would be triumphant, therefore she went home and awaited the call for her diagnosis. A week later the Doctor's secretary phoned and asked Mrs. Kensington "to come in and speak with her physician," hence, for support, her husband accompanied her when they received the terrible news that "she had developed breast cancer!"

Mrs. Kensington decided to break the news to all her children at once and gathered them at the house for Sunday supper the following week. Danielle had not visited their home since she diagnosed the cancer and, while bringing the food to the table, Deloris was asked about her by one of the Kensington children. The mention of the little girl compelled Mrs. Kensington to reflect on the lifesaving information she received from Danielle, so she ordered everyone to "drop their utensils and step away from the table until she returned!" Despite the protest from her hungry mob, Mrs. Kensington left and drove to Daliah's apartment and invited both mother and daughter to join her family for dinner. With everyone Mrs. Kensington wanted present, the food was brought back to the table, before she blessed the meal and allowed them to finally partake. After watching the fellowship among her loved ones while they joked and demolished the food, the hostess took the floor and bravely revealed her reason for the gathering. The Kensington children were sympathetically saddened and shocked by the news as they flocked to their mother and expressed their sentiments, but the Devow females were already aware of the diagnosis.

The festive atmosphere around the dinner table changed and, despite all of Mrs. Kensington's efforts to convince her children that she would survive, they knew the dangers of cancer and understood there was a distinct possibility they could lose their mother. The outpouring of emotions saddened Judge Kensington, who excused himself from the table and went outside to smoke his pipe. Deloris helped to comfort the youngsters and enlightened them on the importance of staying positive for their mother at such a fragile time. Mrs. Kensington got treated like royalty thereafter by her children, as even her daughters offered to lift and carry her around the house.

Later that evening after the festivities had settled, Mrs. Kensington was resting in bed when Danielle walked in. The Kensington's eldest child, Gerald, who no longer resided at home was departing and offered Daliah a ride home, thus she advised Danielle to go inform their hostess that she was leaving.

"Mrs. Kensington, Mrs. Kensington are you awake," Danielle called?

"Hey honey, go close the door and come sit beside me," Mrs. Kensington stated.

Danielle did as instructed, while the Lady of The House sat up and drank some water from a glass on the nightstand. Mrs. Kensington had not taken the time to personally speak with Danielle after hearing such disappointing news, but she was deeply appreciative for the advanced warning.

"When you told me about the lump in my breast, I got very scared because my mother died from breast cancer when I was about your age. But, thanks to you, I have the chance to survive much longer than she did, so I want to say thank you for telling me," said Mrs. Kensington before giving Danielle a huge hug!

"You're welcome!"

"Honey I want for you to do me a big favor, but this will be our little secret?!"

"O.K! What is it?"

"I would like you to look into my future and let me know if I'm going to survive this cancer treatment? This is not something I'd typically ask, but the kids got me all worked up and nervous, so!"

Danielle took Mrs. Kensington's right hand into her left palm and used her right index finger to gently pass along her inner palm until she felt a connecting energy that shocked her eyes closed. Different images passed through Danielle's thoughts of doctor visits, hospital stays, drug treatments, surgical operations, prayers, and sadness, followed by joyous times after regaining a clean bill of health status. Instead of ending the read at that point Danielle wanted to check if the cancer would eventually return, and thus scrolled further into Mrs. Kensington's future. Although she did not detect the cancer returning, the Little Girl saw a tumultuous incident involving kidnappers, which ended with her being taken and the Kensington house getting destroyed by fire. Danielle's entire body trembled as she envisioned herself screaming for her mother and other loved ones who were all caught inside the burning residence.

"Danielle, Danielle, Danielle are you alright honey," enquired Mrs. Kensington with a high-pitched whisper?

Danielle's eyes reopened and she donned a faint smile as if she was simply playing around, before she gave their hostess another hug and slid off the bed. "Gerald said he is going to give mom and me a drive home, so I have to go. But, after the doctors cut off your breast, the cancer won't come back!"

The Palm Reader's prediction caused Mrs. Kensington's eyes to fill with tears and brought with it a comforting state of mind as she watched Danielle exit the room. Knowing what was to come and not being able to change the course of events angered the little girl, who pretended as if all was well while leaving. Whether or not she got kidnapped became irrelevant to Danielle, who knew she must somehow save the lives of the Kensington's and her two favorite ladies. Danielle went home that night and secretly began researching her family history in addition to the Obeah Religion, for which she had to scroll through Underground Websites to find anything noteworthy. There initially was not enough information about the practitioners of Obeah, but the young heir drew a sketch of the symbol on her chest and scanned it into the search bar. It was at that point that the primary website for people who studied and practiced sorcery appeared and revealed everything about the secret cult from where they originated to the size of their organization globally. The more Danielle read about the supernatural mysteries of Obeah the more she lost confidence in saving her loved ones. Therefore, to create an equal field of battle, she began studying and tinkering with Black Magic.

Chapter 14

Even though Madam Devow's age was well beyond the century mark, her physical appearance and agility dictated otherwise, due to her sustained involvement with the paranormal entities from Lucifer's realm. The Devow females had always lived by a strict code of conduct and that entailed "Loyalty above all to their religion," but the defection of Dion's predecessor threatened to destroy their entire organization. Without Danielle present on the date of Dion's expiration to receive her preternatural powers, the force would retire with the Obeah Woman and the arrangement between their family and Satan would be forever broken. Even though Danielle was born to be the recipient of the West Witch's preternatural powers, there existed specific incidents under which she could lose the privilege. Should she encounter an unforeseen death within minutes of Dion's expiration and another heir was in existence, then the presiding Bush Doctor would retain her powers until the baby comes of age.

Mama Devow developed a hatred towards Danielle so that, even if she returned of her own free will, she had no chance of retrieving her birthright. The witch had a terrible habit of talking to herself, and managed to convince herself that to create a dominating spell caster such as herself, she must be the child's sole guardian and teacher. The insubordination of all three Devow females was only punishable by death, but because they lived overseas and had devoted their lives to the worship of God, Dion could not harm them. The bush doctor's binding contract with Lucifer was significantly more important than the loss of any family member, thus she drew up a plot to preserve the integrity of her prehistoric institution.

As the years of her reign dwindled, Dion began developing added wrinkles and gradually became weaker as the time progressed. The plans she developed for the preservation of her empire had to be executed to perfection to gain success, hence she instructed her maid to summon Cynthia Clark, Glen Thompkins and Tyliq Davis. To set her plans into motion the West Witch personally contacted the cancer survivor Mr. Riley and arranged to borrow his private aircraft for a trip to Canada. The business mogul collected the personal information of those traveling and made all the necessary arrangements, before he contacted the Obeah healer with the confirmation and flight itinerary. With the traveling arrangements handled, the West Witch went to her Spell Chamber and conjured up a special magic potion that induced unconsciousness, then waited for her guest to arrive.

Officer Thompkins was the first to arrive and brought to the West Witch, who was inside her Private Study. Madam Dion Devow was seated behind her desk sipping on a glass of red wine and instructed her maid "to pour the officer a generous drink of Wray & Nephew, Overproof White Rum before exiting." Once everything got organized and Barbara left the room Dion proceeded to explain the reason for summoning Glen, as he sat comfortably and smoked a small Marijuana Joint while drinking the liquor.

"You go take a week off from work for vacation purposes… and I'm sending you to Quebec, Canada to bring back my child! As for her mother and grandmother who thief her away, I want them to pay with their lives for their betrayal! I want them to burn, you hear me!? You schedule to leave in three days with two other people, so make arrangements and, on the date of you flight, my driver will transport you all to the private plane."

"How we supposed to find this girl?"

"The Black Crows will find you at the appropriate time and show you the way. It is important that the young lady gets sedated before reaching here, but make absolute sure that she is not harmed! And don't forget to carry your passport!"

"Yes Ma'am," stated Glen who exited thereafter!

***

Cynthia arrived approximately an hour after Glen departed and met with the Madam inside the same room. When Cynthia entered behind the maid, Dion, who rarely smoked was stuffing Tobacco into her pipe, which she then lit ablaze and smoked uninterruptedly. Personal clients of the Bush Doctor were aware to never interrupt her and only respond when spoken to, therefore Cynthia simply sat quietly and watched her spiritual advisor indulge. For the first three minutes of her visit the witch neglected to mention a word, thus Cynthia, who was already concerned about the reason for being summoned, grew increasingly nervous. It had been well documented by residents in the parish that disgracing Mama Devon meant damnation, therefore Cynthia nervously prayed she had done nothing deserving of being punished.

The West Witch always appeared angry and malicious; therefore, her client obtained a cramp in her stomach through fear, but relief ensued once the old woman slid her a small pouch containing Butterfly Needles and a tube filled with the serum she concocted earlier. Cynthia unzipped the pouch and looked at the contents inside, following which, the Obeah woman advised her of her plot.

"In three days, I'm sending you and two others to Quebec, Canada. Your duties during this trip is to keep sedated the young lady I'm sending you all for. Make sure you inject her with 30 cc of the ointment inside the pouch once she is captured and every three hours thereafter!... Am I understood!"

"Yes Ma'am!"

"You may go and advise whoever you need to; and I'll have a driver bring you all to the airport when its time to leave. Be sure to bring your passport!"

"Yes Ma'am!"

***

Tyliq, who lived much further away in Montego Bay, arrived at 6:15 P.M. but had to wait an additional 20 minutes while Madam Devow finished with a client. The instant the bush doctor summoned Tyliq, he fell under a trance and became less interactive at work before he walked off the job. Even though he left work without advising his boss, followed by a lengthy taxi drive to the country, Tyliq remained remarkably focused when approached by the witch's assistant. Barbara led her mistress' guest to the Spell Room where the Obeah practitioner was busy assembling the products, she would need to perform the ceremony.

"You will have to remove all your clothing," instructed Barbara!

At the sight of Tyliq's naked muscular frame and appealing masculinity, Barbara inhaled a deep breath as she collected his clothes, folded them, and placed them on a table in the corner. The sexually enticed maid grabbed Tyliq's derriere as she directed him towards the center of the room and had him lay down on his back, before she exited and properly sealed the entrance. Mama Devow, who never indulged in idle conversational dialog with her clients and always wore a serious expression on her face, walked over with several items on a tray and placed it beside her client.

"In three days, you and two others will be travelling to Quebec, Canada to kidnap Danielle and bring her back here to me," Mama Devow implied!

THE DEVIL'S CONCUBINE

"But I don't own a Canadian Visa Mama Devow," Tyliq argued.

"All the arrangements are being handled… a driver will pick you up and get you to the plane. Just be sure to bring your passport," Mama Devow instructed!

"Yes Ma'am," Tyliq answered!

The mention of his abducted daughter and thoughts of her once desirable mother sent undisclosed chills through Tyliq, who could still recall the day he returned home to an empty house. It had been 18 plus years of anxiety for Tyliq who had two other children at home, but regularly dreamt about their eldest sister. With her guest resting comfortably on the ground inside her Circle of Realms, the Obeah practitioner took a small bottle containing the magic potion used to transform individuals and gave it to Tyliq for him to drink. Without hesitation her client slowly drank the fluid while she lit a red candle and dropped the hot wax around his body as she chanted in her African tongue. As if instructed to by the hostess, the Nyabinghi Drummer began slowly beating the drums in the background to an ancient traditional beat. Madam Devow stood by Tyliq's head with her fingers interlocked and prayed to her God with her eyes closed, then maintained the posture as she hummed like a Buddhist Monk for a few minutes thereafter. Following her meditative aspect of the ceremony the Obeah woman collected a jar containing a golden powdery substance from the tray and sprinkled it across Tyliq's entire body.

"I call upon thee to do my bidding, Oh mighty and powerful Rolling Calf. Enter this vessel and transform him as your replica, then lay dormant until I summon thee to trample and burn my enemies!"

Tyliq started cringing and screaming in pain as if his skin was engulfed in flames while his muscles expanded enormously beyond that of any power weightlifter. Different areas of his body got swollen and exhibited massive muscle tones then quickly shrunk and his hands and feet changed to hooves before returning normal. The Witch's subject grabbed his head and grinded his teeth with his eyes tightly closed as his cranium expanded and transformed to resemble that of a bull. Once the horns began puncturing through his skull Tyliq's eyes flashed wide open, to which he groaned out loud in anguish and spun flames through his mouth. At the end of the ceremony, a notably possessed Tyliq simply got up from the floor and got dressed, then bowed in respect and exited once Barbara opened the door.

***

Three days later, the West Witch's personal chauffeur picked up Cynthia first on route to their flight, then Officer Thompkins and finally Tyliq. Following the introductions between Glen and Cynthia neither of them spoke with the other throughout the duration of the trip, thus the trend continued after they got Tyliq and acknowledged each other. Their private flight originated in Montego Bay and was scheduled to travel directly to a small airport in Gatineau, Quebec, where the plane would anchor until its passengers and cargo was ready to return. The chauffeur drove to a private entrance at the Sangster International Airport and provided the guard with an access pass and was allowed to drive directly to their private plane. The plane attendants handled their luggage and allowed them to greet Mr. Riley who awaited them at the base of the aircraft. Once they got introduced Mr. Riley welcomed the three kidnappers aboard his private jet and within minutes, they were taxing down the runway.

Chapter 15

Danielle slid out of bed the following morning and developed a light-headed sensation while walking to the bathroom. She stumbled against the dresser and grabbed a hold to avoid tumbling to the floor while she regained her composure before continuing on. The heir to the West Witch's kingdom knew instantly that something was wrong and decided to stay home from school for precautionary reasons. While looking at her reflection through the medicine chest mirror, Danielle saw flashes of the images she had repeatedly envisioned since the day she read Mrs. Kensington's palm. There were minor differences between her regular hallucinations and the visions she saw that day, which led her to speculate that the plot against her life was imminent.

Daliah had long completed her university studies and worked for the

MAMA DEVOW

Youth's Services Department in Gatineau as a social worker, who only devoted her time to helping the minors on her case load, family and church. The house phone rang and startled Danielle from her hallucination, so she rushed to answer, knowing that was about the time her mother normally phoned to ensure she had awakened for school. Both ladies spoke briefly during which Danielle refrained from mentioning anything about missing school or her temporary dizzy spell, to avoid alarming her mother who would immediately rush home.

"Hello mom!"

"Did you climb out of bed yet?"

"Already did, I was about to take a shower and get ready."

"Ok well have a nice day… and what are we eating for dinner this evening!?"

"Oh Mrs. Kensington called and invited us to dinner; so, you can just meet me there after you're done at work."

"That sounds like a plan. I wonder what they have on the menu tonight!? Wish I could phone mother to pry, but I'm swamped with work for the day, so see you later and be careful! I love you!"

"Yes mom, love you too!"

When Danielle decided to study the practice of Obeah, she first became a member of their online congregation, then secretly started acquiring ancient literatures that contained demonic spells and examples on how to cast such incantations. Mama Devow's usage of the crows as spies and how to disrupt whatever images they transferred back was the first mandate of sorcery that Danielle tackled. To test her spell-casting abilities, the apprentice followed the specific instructions given in one of her training manuals and created an obfuscation for the watchful birds to transmit. The spell tricked the crows into believing they were watching Danielle study for school on her bed, during which she exited through her front door and unknowingly recorded them from below. Throughout the ensuing years the young witch practiced developing her mystical powers and believed she could ward off any adversary, therefore she did as she normally did and got prepared for school.

Once behind closed doors inside the bathroom Danielle used her magic to visualize her captors in order to decipher their plans on accomplishing their mission. It was impossible for the crows to see inside the bathroom due to the drapes at the window, hence that allowed the aspiring Bush Doctor the ability to operate. Danielle had built a hidden compartment inside the wall of the cupboard underneath the sink where she hid her Satanic artifacts and literature, thus she collected the items she needed to perform her "spirit out of body" technique and assembled them on the counter.

To begin, she laid a black worshipping mat containing a circle of the "Cycle of Life," which was the Devil's chart that proved he had conquered the entire world. Around the edges of the circle are hundreds of governing seals from great human empires throughout history, with the demonic symbol of Lucifer in the middle to illustrate to whom they offered godly devotion. There was a pouch containing six candles, each of which she lit and positioned at specific areas around the Cycle of Life, before she got completely undressed and stepped in the center of the mat.

"My Lord in the Realm of Darkness, acknowledge my prayers and grant my request," repeated Danielle six times before she started humming with a moderate pitch!?

Suddenly the room felt as if all the oxygen had gotten sucked out and Danielle was floating in space as a voice pierced through the darkness. "What is it that you seek?"

The thundering tone startled Danielle, who felt tremors as if there was an earthquake erupting. "I wish… to float about like a free spirit?"

"Ahhh," lamented the voice as if contemplating how to respond! "Very well, you will be allowed one earth hour… but make sure you are back inside your vessel before the hour strikes, or you will be forever trapped in the realm of the dead!"

At the conclusion of their conversation, Danielle felt her life-force detach itself from her body, where she was floating in mid air while staring down at her anatomy. As fascinated as she became with her transparent appearance the thought of remaining as such should the time awarded expire forced her to focus on the task ahead, hence Danielle glided through the closed door and left her body frozen like a mannequin. The intrusive eyes of the crows that sat on the Hydro Electrical Wire and along tree branches were pasted at her bedroom window as Danielle unknowingly snuck by and went about her affairs. The transformation gave the young apprentice supernatural capabilities whereby she developed the ability to track the kidnappers like a bloodhound. Even though the "Spirit Out of Body" technique proved efficient at getting by the crows unnoticed in addition to geographically locating the team of abductors, Danielle hated not being abled to smell Earth's aromas or feel the breeze against her skin as she would if she was inside her anatomy.

When Mr. Riley's private plane arrived at the Gatineau Executive Airport in Quebec, a pair of Canadian Immigration Officers boarded to inspect the travelers' documents and cargo. None of the aircraft owner's companions were legally supposed to depart the aircraft without proper visas, but the millionaire bribed both inspectors and paid them five thousand dollars each for a 48-hour visit. Mr. Riley provided the kidnappers with a fully furnished condominium for lodging but opted instead to rent a penthouse suite at the Hilton Hotel attached to the infamous Casino du Lac Leamy. Should anything unforeseen transpire the millionaire did not wish to get entangled with the group, therefore he spent all his time playing high stakes poker and enjoying himself until they contacted him to leave.

Danielle arrived at the condominium and found Glen Thompkins inside the dinning room on the ground floor with a Caucasian male gun dealer. Along the 12-mile journey between her house and the condo, Danielle went by several properties from which she sensed evil spirits, but none of them felt as injurious as those inside the kidnappers' dwelling. Every few minutes, a huge bang sounded on the upper floor as if someone was intentionally breaking furniture against the walls, however neither Glen nor his associate behaved remotely concerned. Both Glen and the dealer were seated around the dinning table conducting a sales transaction over seven hand pistols and three assault rifles. Glen inspected all nine weapons before selecting two Beretta 92FS with extra clips for each and a box of bullets. At the conclusion of their meeting, Danielle floated up to the second floor where Cynthia was lying on her bed talking to her husband who was back in Jamaica with their daughter. The Obeah apprentice grew surprised at discovering she was able to read Cynthia's thoughts, which meant that she was not under the mind control of Mme Dion Devow. Danielle's attempt to visit with Tyliq was not as successful, as her demon-possessed-father felt her life force enter his domain and moved violently towards her. During the attack, the intrusive apprentice could only see the massive fiery frame of the Rolling Calf moving towards her, therefore she quickly vanished through the floor boarding before the beast grabbed her. The destructive beast within Tyliq prevented him from resting, hence he returned to smashing furniture and punching through walls until he grew fatigued. Danielle quickly glided downstairs and was about to exit the dwelling when she overheard Glen on the telephone telling someone that, "even though they could only be there for another day and a half they should be ready to return to the islands by morning."

Throughout her upbringing thus far, Danielle had always been accustomed to people being intimidated by her, but, for the first time in her existence, she genuinely felt threatened. The entire trip took 39 minutes, following which she returned home disheartened and affixed her life-force with her anatomy. Once her respiratory system returned to normal the Obeah apprentice opened the hot water faucet inside the shower and climbed in, then stood under the soothing water flow and contemplated how to proceed. Danielle wanted to protect all the people she cared about with every resource available and assumed that being with an officer of the court who could have the entire police force at his house in seconds was her best option, but after seeing the mythical Rolling Calf firsthand and knowing its efficiency at tracking its prey, she felt almost defeated.

Daliah was able to dress Danielle relatively conservatively prior to her decision to study Black Magic, where she totally transformed her style in fashion. The Aspiring Witch's colorful wardrobe changed instantly as she began exclusively wearing dark colored clothing, in addition to severing her ties with the church siting bigotry towards her by the other members as her excuse. To deter her mother from becoming suspicious and eventually discover her involvement in the Demonic Arts, Danielle attended school regularly and maintained exemplary grades, lived in tranquility like her guardians without raising unwanted attention and demonstrated absolute disgust towards witchcraft.

Deloris would recount the stories of their ancestors during her sleepovers and made Danielle pledge "to never consider the island of her birth as a vacation destination, especially if the West Witch still had breath in her body." In order to break their family's contract with the Devil Deloris knew they must keep Danielle from pursuing her birthright and return to dethrone the reigning witch, therefore she lied to her granddaughter and told her that "Dion wanted only to kill her and steal her powers!" Even though Danielle was extremely fond of the ancient day stories and would drift back into time while her grandmother spoke, her vision of the future was far different from the life her guardians wished and would have killed for. There were several instances during her upbringing where Danielle detected that should she have decided to rejoin Mama Devow then her life would be in danger, thus she hid her aspirations and developed her skills in secret.

The crows were accustomed to Danielle spending hours inside the bathroom while she bathed, therefore no alarms were raised during her time alone. There were always at least three crows on watch even when a freshly killed caucus got discovered at which most of them would leave to feed. Danielle exited the bathroom in her bathrobe and climbed back into bed with her book assignment and began reading. After three minutes of allowing the birds to intensely watch her, Danielle twirled her right hand in a circular motion at them and said, "see me as I am until you are awakened!" The spell that the apprentice witch casted paralyzed the birds' focus on her in the bed and allowed Danielle to dress and go about her affairs without being pursued and documented.

When Danielle arrived on the Kensington's property and walked around to the back of the house where Deloris could often be found inside the kitchen, she observed her grandmother giving a Caucasian male an envelope enclosed with $100 bills and two pictures. The man was dressed completely in army fatigues with Timberland boots, a Toronto Blue Jays baseball cap and resembled an off-duty soldier, but as he lifted his sunglasses to his face Danielle caught a glimpse of his eyes. From their momentary eye contact Danielle experienced a premonition where she saw the man's right eye spying through a rifle scope at her before he pulled the trigger. However, the vision stopped once his eyes vanished behind his sunglasses. Deloris was noticeably startled by the sight of her granddaughter who kept a close watch on the suspicious visitor as he left. When asked who the strange man was, Deloris again lied to her granddaughter and responded that "he was a delivery man for the Kensington's," but the young apprentice had grown to trust her instincts and thus suspected otherwise.

Chapter 16

Madam Devow locked herself in the center of her Reading Chamber and whispered a silent prayer to her Lord before she began meditating, which led to her telepathically contacting with the birds she employed to watch her successor. The sudden linkage of minds awakened the crows from the spell under which Danielle placed them, therefore the West Witch noted firsthand that she was missing. Dion became enraged at the fact that the birds somehow foiled their assignment and allowed Danielle to leave unnoticed, hence she ordered them to 'spread out and find the young apprentice immediately!' With Glen Thompkins and her extradition team ready to carry out their mission it was imperative that the birds locate Danielle and relay her location to the kidnappers who only had a few hours left on Canadian soil.

THE DEVIL'S CONCUBINE

The Crows looked at each other as if coordinating their strategy before they all flew off in different directions. The birds individually went to every recorded destination Danielle had ever visited as they combed through the entire region of Aylmer and the Gatineau surrounding areas. For the next 10 hours the crows searched intensely for Danielle to no avail, sending up to four separate patrols by locations to ensure she had not returned there. The more time that elapsed off the clock the more desperate the birds became. Knowing the witch they served could sentence them to unimaginable horrors they expanded their field of search to include public buses, taxies, parks and even her former church. Danielle spent her entire afternoon inside her grandmother's bedroom with the blinds drawn shut to prevent all exterior spies from seeing her.

To advise her mother of her whereabouts, Danielle sent her a text message stating that "she was at the Kensington's house and would wait there for her after she had finished working." Not wanting to create any turmoil between her mother and Danielle, Daliah neglected to enquire why was she at her grandmother's instead of class and simply responded OK? On her way to the Kensington's that evening Daliah stopped at the SAQ liquor dispensary in Hull and purchased two bottles of her mother's favorite white wine, plus a third bottle for the homeowners. While waiting for the bus thereafter, the Alpha Crow involved in the search for Danielle noticed Daliah at the bus stop and pitched on the Hydro electrical wire as it began surveying her. Once Daliah's bus arrived and she climbed aboard, the bird began pursuing and trailed the public transport until she dismounted at her destination. At no point along the journey did Daliah ever get the sense that she was being tracked by the crow, which knew she was an intricate part of her daughter's life, not to mention they rarely separated.

Three crows had already searched the premises before moving on to look elsewhere, but the Alpha Crow was positive that Daliah would lead it to her daughter and thus stayed with her. When Daliah rang the doorbell Mrs. Kensington graciously answered and welcomed her with a huge hug, at which she presented her mother's employer with the bottle of Chardonnay. During their casual chat Mrs. Kensington revealed that Danielle had indicated she wasn't feeling well; and thus, allowed to rest inside the quiet serenity of her grandmother's room. At the mention of Danielle's complaint of illness Daliah immediately became concerned knowing her daughter had never once gotten sick throughout her entire upbringing. Respect was an important trait to her mother as a maid, therefore she located Mr. Kensington inside his private study and appropriately greeted him before looking in on her daughter.

The Alpha Crow watched Daliah and flew from window to window as she made her way through the lower tier of the house, until she entered Deloris' dark room and completely vanished from sight. While inside the room with her daughter Daliah checked her forehead, neck, and other areas for signs of fever but found nothing wrong, yet still Danielle claimed, "she had a massive headache and felt ill." Daliah spent 10 minutes inside the room before emerging to rejoin her mother and the people who made it possible for them to begin their lives in a foreign country after they fled Jamaica. Although Danielle neglected to materialize with her mother, the crow became suspicious and presumed she was inside the dark room, so it pitched on a pine tree limb in the back yard from which it could clearly see the room door.

There were still two of the Kensington's children living at home who were locked inside their rooms. The lady of the house, after opening the door, had gone on to the arrangement of a breast cancer fundraiser she was involved with, thereby she was glued to the telephone discussing important issues with her helpers. By the time Daliah rejoined Deloris, her mother was packing the dishes from supper inside the dishwasher and tidying the kitchen, but had prepared a plate for her daughter who sat and ate on a high stool by the counter.

"Hey mama how has your day been?"

"Not bad honey… the arthritis still acting up but overall I'm fine! How are things at work?"

"Same old crap everyday it's like fighting a losing battle at times… But what happen with D, she seemed fine when I talked to her this morning?"

"I can't really say, she just said she don't feel well and she wanted to lay down so I close the shutters and let her sleep!"

"Did she eat any at all?"

"Yes, I made her some soup and Mrs. Kensington brought it in for her."

After they finished inside the kitchen, both ladies retired to Deloris' quarters, which was the last room down a short hallway, where they had the laundry area, a pantry, the interior door that led to the garage and the maid's bathroom, directly across from her dwelling. Daliah checked Danielle's temperature again to ensure she hadn't developed a fever, before they began watching the evening lineup of television programs that the maid routinely tuned into. One of Deloris' passion during her leisure time was to crochet and would knit fabulous bedtime shoes and sweaters for the people she cared about. Deloris was most comfortably crocheting in her rocking chair, which allowed Daliah to lay beside her daughter on the bed. Danielle slept soundly while her guardians who both watched identical programs each night elaborated on every aspects of the shows. At 11:00 P.M. Daliah decided to return home alone without Danielle who asked to remain under the care of her grandmother, considering her mother had to report into work in the morning. Instead of summoning a taxi Daliah decided to walk home because of the short distance and started gathering her personal items to leave. Danielle arose from the bed and left the room to use the bathroom across the hall which inherently allowed the Alpha Crow to see her, thus it immediately flew off in the kidnappers' direction.

Despite the late hour Mrs. Kensington was still engaged in her fundraising activities but took time to pass by Deloris' room and check in on Danielle. The West Witch's heir used the restroom then returned to her grandmother's bedroom and was about to leap back into bed when she noticed the lady of the house standing beside Deloris. There was a special bond between Mrs. Kensington and Danielle that prevented the young Obeah apprentice from simply walking by her. Therefore, despite her pretense of illness, the aspiring witch went over and hugged her. Daliah who was preparing to leave felt somewhat snubbed by her daughter who didn't relay the same affections to her, but she understood the close relationship both females shared and smiled at the gesture. As both ladies embraced Danielle began experiencing futuristic visions where she saw Mrs. Kensington screaming in pain inside her burning house. Believing that she could remain hidden until the abduction team left Canadian soil, Danielle pushed the lady of the house aside and started screaming, "No, no, no, no, no!"

"What is it honey, what's wrong," Deloris asked!

"I tried Grandma… but they are about to find us," Danielle answered!

"Who Danielle, who is about to find us," Mrs. Kensington shouted?

"Madam Dion Devow's lynch-men," whispered Deloris who was noticeably trembling!

Everyone inside the room fell dumbstruck by the report, therefore Mrs. Kensington telephoned the police.

***

The Alpha Crow pitched on the window ledge outside the main floor of the condominium and tapped its beak on the glass, which alerted Glen Thompkins that it had found their target. Glen ran upstairs and moved to knock Cynthia's door, but surprisingly she walked out with the pouch given to her by their boss. A knock on their male counterpart's door would not prove as successful, as Tyliq's condition gradually changed.

"Tyliq, let's go the spotter crow is at the window," Glen declared!

"I will find the place myself," stated a rumbling bass toned voice that sounded different from Tyliq's!

"Don't be ridiculous man you can't find it without the crow," Glen argued!

"I said…go," threatened the thundering tone!

Glen slowly backed away from the door sensing that whatever was behind it was about to break through and he felt positively assured that it would not be Tyliq. Both Cynthia and he climbed into a borrowed Range Rover Sport inside the garage then rolled out with the crow flying directly ahead of them. The Rolling Calf demon that Madam Devow placed inside Tyliq was not a creature that one could contain for more than 24 hours, therefore, three minutes after his team members departed the transformed flame engulfed beast broke through the back wall of the condo leaving a gaping hole. Fire could be seen burning inside the condo as engulfed construction materials fell beside the creature, which sniffed the air around before it scampered off. The neighbor who lived behind the condominium was fixing himself a drink in his kitchen, when saw the fiery glowing Rolling Calf. Hence, the man slowly poured the liquid down the sink drain and walked away, believing it was prompting him to see things that wasn't there.

Cynthia and Glen arrived at the Kensington's house to find a patrolling officer parked in front with his sirens flashing. The Officer was engaged in a conversation with Mrs. Kensington and the other ladies at the door, while the crow circled overhead then pitched on the roof to properly identify their location to target. The Rolling Calf stayed off the main roads and made its own passage along the inner shores of the Ottawa River, from which it snuck into the Judge's back yard. The crow seated on the roof of the house clarified that the Rolling Calf was at the correct address, therefore, to immediately empty the structure the beast started setting fire to the rear and left side of the house. At the sight of the flames Glen drove up to the house pretending to be a concerned neighbor who was trying to warn the homeowners, and intentionally created a massive panic amongst the dwellers. Huge flames began lighting up the night's skies prior to a deafening explosion from the gas tanks used by the furnace, which destroyed Deloris' room and the entire rear section of the house.

"Fire, Fire! The whole house on fire," yelled Glen!

"Get out of the house now everyone," instructed the Officer!

"No…my children and husband are in there," Mrs. Kensington shouted and ran back into the burning house!

Deloris, Daliah and Danielle all hugged each other and went with the officer who was simultaneously transmitting the latest occurrence to his dispatcher, when Glen shot him four times with one of his firearms. The bullets pitched the officer to the ground in the headlights of his patrol car where he was coughing up blood before he went silent. All three generations of Devow women cuddled tightly and appeared as if they were about to surrender peacefully, when Danielle broke away and went for the officer's gun. Even though she had never fired a weapon before Danielle inspected the handgun in the bright headlight and clicked it off safety, then aimed it at the kidnapper and squeezed the trigger several times.

Glen was forced to retreat behind his vehicle for safety as bullets ripped into the structure of the Range Rover. The Heir to Mama Devow's throne, knew that the kidnappers could not hurt her and wanted desperately to save the lives of her family. Cynthia believed that she had not been seen by any of the females and could thus sneak around behind Danielle and inject her with the serum given to her by the architect behind the scenes. With the injection at hand, she slowly crept around behind the cruiser, and remarkably came within four feet of Danielle, when the Obeah apprentice spun around and touched her directly in the center of the forehead with her index finger and said, "settle yourself woman!"

Cynthia froze like a mannequin and went completely irresponsive with her eyes wide open during which Danielle chatted with her in a foreign language that no one else understood. Deloris and Daliah became astonished by Danielle's use of the ancient Black Art as they watched her cast a spell on Cynthia. Glen was not in position to observe the incident between Cynthia and Danielle, but utilized those precious few seconds where their armed target's gun went silent to change his fortune. Instead of walking towards Danielle who forced the cop killer to retreat, her guardians remained by the side of the cruiser which allowed Glen to sneak around behind them. Glen grabbed Daliah from behind by the neck and used the same hand to grab a hold of Deloris' blouse, then aimed his 9 mm to the back of Danielle's mother's head.

"Hey, drop the gun or else I kill your mother right now," threatened Glen who began noticing neighbors coming out and wanted the standoff to end!

Danielle held the gun to Cynthia's head and began looking around for their third companion, knowing that he was a viable adversary.

"I will kill this bitch and you if you hurt my mother," Danielle answered!

"Help us," begged Mrs. Kensington who was struggling with her husband draped over her shoulder?

As they walked out the front entrance to the house the Rolling Calf came through the inferno from behind and pierced both its horns through the Kensington couple, then stood on the verandah with their bodies dangling from its horns. With Mrs. Kensington squirming for life in front the blazing house the premonition Danielle had of her came to fruition, so she screamed out in anger and grabbed her stomach in pain. Before long, the creature rested its sights on Deloris and Daliah and thus discarded of its previous kills by tossing the bodies back into the fiery flames. Watching the people who she held in the highest regards get assassinated enraged Danielle, who cast a second spell that would enable the officer's bullets to kill the Rolling Calf.

"I consecrate these bullets to be dipped in the blood of the bull who is my Lord Lucifer that they may send this abomination back into the crevices of the underworld," Danielle then bit her lip and spat the blood from her mouth onto the weapon and aimed it at the Rolling Calf, that was barreling towards her guardians!

Two shots fired from the weapon and struck the beast which caused it to slow and stagger, yet still it was intent on killing its targets even at Glen's expense. The impact from Danielle's first two demonically engineered bullets caused the Rolling Calf to uncloak so its human form became visible for a few seconds, thus allowing Daliah the chance to see Tyliq. The creature properly regained its balance and again charged at both defectors, who were still being held by Glen and unable to escape the assault. Despite the dangers involving her mother and herself Daliah yelled out at Danielle to prevent her from further injuring the attacking Rolling Calf.

"Danielle he is your father don't kill him," screamed Daliah, however the aspiring witch shot the beast twice thereafter!

The sudden flinch and outburst by Daliah startled Glen, who accidentally shot her in the back of the head. That momentary jest of shock caused Danielle to lose focus of the spell she had casted against Cynthia, which allowed the kidnapper to awaken. Cynthia was unsure of what happened, nevertheless she immediately injected the serum into the back of their target's neck. The fluid travelled through Danielle's bloodstream and affected her nerve system, causing her to drop the weapon and eventually faint to the ground. Although the targeted female's body got paralyzed her eyes remained wide open allowing her to see everything that transpired, but still she could not speak. Glen quickly picked up Danielle and threw her on the back seat before helping his retransformed bloody accomplice into their Range Rover, then quickly drove away from the neighborhood.

The moment they drove away, emergency personnel from the police, ambulance and fire department arrived and attended to those on the scene in addition to the burning house. With such a huge debacle involving the kidnapping of a female plus the killings of a provincial court judge, his wife, their two children and an officer of the law, Glen instructed Cynthia to contact Mr. Riley and advise him "they were ready to leave immediately!" The bloodied registered nurse, who had fought to save her teammate's life from the moment she entered the vehicle did as instructed, with Danielle looking on with tears in her eyes. Arrangements were made for them to drive directly to the airstrip at which they landed, however tragically along the way Tyliq succumbed to his injuries.

When they reached the Gatineau Exclusive Airport, Glen drove directly into a private hanger where the aircraft was being prepared for departure. The pilot was doing his personal inspection of the aircraft while the maintenance crew stocked the plane with the necessary amenities. Glen first transported Danielle aboard the plane and buckled her into a seat before he attended to Tyliq or any other business. By the time Glen returned from inside the aircraft Cynthia had created a body bag made with two ex-large Glade Bags and Duct Tape provided by a member of the Grounds Crew. Glen made two members of the Maintenance Crew take Tyliq's body and place it safely inside the cargo area underneath the plane, before both Cynthia and he boarded. Mr. Riley arrived a few minutes later and handsomely paid everyone for their silence before running onto the plane, following which the hostess closed the door and they began rolling out of the hanger. Within 25 minutes of the kidnappers' arrival at the airport, the private jet was taxiing down the runway before it took to the skies on route to the Caribbean Island of Jamaica.

Their mission was a resounding success, but to avoid leaving any incriminating evidence on foreign soil, Tyliq's corpse was brought instead of burying it at some questionable location. Secrecy was a pivotal factor in Madam Devow's business, therefore should they get caught and the extracted bullets from Tyliq examined, the witch's plot could eventually get exposed. It was impossible for them to land the private jet at any of the major airports where immigration officials would find the body upon inspection, so they contacted the West Witch and advised her of their dilemma. Dion Devow, who had multitudes of contacts across the island, advised them to proceed to the Negril Aerodrome which was a much smaller airstrip located in the Parish of Hanover, where suitable arrangements were being coordinated.

When the private aircraft landed, the pilot received instructions from the Airplane Traffic Tower to bring the plane to an unregulated area of the Aerodrome. Flights that originated out of the country were authorized by the Jamaican Air Traffic Control to undergo inspections by immigration agents prior to anyone exiting the plane, but, uncharacteristically, when they landed there were no available immigration agents on location. The plane came to a halt beside Madam Devow's personal vehicle and a crew of engineers was waiting to quickly unload the dead body and everyone involved with the kidnapping. There were five men sent by the West Witch who all appeared as if they were under some sort of trance yet were remarkably efficient at their duties. Danielle had to be carried off by Glen who kept her face covered for precautionary reasons and climbed into the awaiting vehicle with Cynthia, while the helpers placed Tyliq's body in the trunk before they drove away and went directly to Mama Devow's estate.

Chapter 17

Barbara was placed in charge of Danielle because her employer could not have any form of contact with her successor. As Dion's long-time maid, Barbara had met and nursed a few of the witch's newly born siblings, but she never got the opportunity to meet Danielle. For them to keep their kidnapped victim under sedation an injection of the serum that was given to Cynthia had to be administered every six hours. Food was given intravenously through an injection considering the paralyzed state the young heir was in. Danielle was kept inside a guest bedroom down the hall from Dion's room, which was adequately equipped with its own bath and amenities except for a telephone. Dion reveled in secrecy and disclosed her affairs to absolutely no one even Barbara her closest servant, hence the maid knew absolutely nothing about the female she was placed in charge of.

THE DEVIL'S CONCUBINE

The only time Barbara was able to get away from Mama Devow for a short period of time was when she got sent out on errands by her employer at which the chauffeur would drive her to and from the location. Wherever she went to represent the most revered Bush Doctor in the West Indies the people with whom she dealt were quite aware of who she was, therefore, nobody dared to interfere or disrupt her business transactions. The people throughout the community were so scared of Mama Devow that they abstained from even discussing her when her representatives were within the vicinity, fearing they might inform the witch. Although there were unconfirmed reports of Danielle's kidnapping circulating throughout the town, Barbara incredibly heard nothing of it despite the fact she lived in the house where the kidnapped victim was being held.

Madam Devow summoned Barbara late one night and advised her to inform the chauffeur "to prepare her private vehicle for departure!" Within minutes Dion's sparkling clean black limousine was parked in front of the house so she walked out covered with a black cloak and climbed in through the chauffeur held door.

"Anywhere in particular tonight Madam," asked the Chauffeur?

"Cruise around the town," instructed Dion.

"Yes Madam!"

The chauffeur drove around the town for nearly thirty minutes while the West Witch closed her eyes and meditated in the back of the car. Madam Devow remained incoherent as they travelled south on Darling Street approaching Lewis Street, when she suddenly popped open her eyes and instructed her chauffeur to "head over to the Burger King on Great George Street!" The driver was aware that the Obeah woman was extremely particular about her diet and thus never partook of fast foods, but regardless the request, he was devoted to serving the witch. While stationed in the Burger King's parking lot inside their tinted limousine with the engine off, both the chauffeur and Dion watched as a Suzuki motorcyclist pulled into the parking and met with two other males.

The men appeared as if they were conducting some sort of drug transaction but after they transferred items the biker who collected the funds realized that a majority of the money was fake. An argument ensued amongst the three men that quickly escalated into a fight wherein the two friends withdrew knives and attempted to stab the biker. The motorcyclist wisely backed away from the attacking men and eased a Glock 20SF 10MM off his hip and fired four shots at them, striking each man twice in the stomach. While maneuvering away from his attackers and arming himself the cyclist unknowingly dropped his cell phone, which slid into a dark corner close to the restaurant. There were no other witnesses to the tragedy inside the parking lot therefore the shooter shoved his weapon into his pocket, reclaimed his property and rode away on his motorcycle.

Mama Devow's limousine trailed the rider south along Great George Street towards Ricketts Street where he continued straight ahead, but instead of pursuing the rider the witch's vehicle turned right on Ricketts and drove to Hudson Street. By the time the motorcyclist arrived at his house on Hudson Street the limousine was parked in front his destination, hence arrogantly he rode up to the vehicle and used his weapon to knock on the driver's window. The rear window rolled down and frightened the rider who spun around and aimed his firearm at Dion, but could not manage to pull the trigger as her eyes hypnotized him.

"Peter Myers... I alone know your purpose in life," Mama Devow stated!

The words resonated with the young man whose eyes brightened like he won the lottery. "Please guide me Mother Lady?"

"Park your bike and get in the car," Mama Devow instructed!

Peter did as ordered and climbed into the front cabin with the chauffeur, who confiscated his firearm without any objections then drove directly to the estate. When they reached the White House, the hypnotized guest followed Madam Devow inside and waited by the foot of the stairs at the snap of her fingers, while she retrieved a magical potion from her Cabinet of Medicines. After attending to the door Barbara stood by the immobilized visitor whose handsome demeanor and muscular physique enticed her to lustfully caress his chest and biceps. The instant she heard Dion coming, Barbara stopped fondling Peter and pretended as if she only stood guard, hence which the Obeah practitioner gave the young man the potion to drink. Once Peter finished consuming the potion Madam Devow whispered instructions in his ears then stood aside while he climbed the stairs leading to the bedroom area. Peter went directly to Danielle's bedroom where the paralyzed female laid motionless on the bed and indiscriminately proceeded to rape her. The entire ordeal took less than five minutes but felt like an eternity to Danielle who was heavily sedated and could not move but understood exactly what was being done to her. With his duties complete Peter got driven back to his house where the chauffeur returned his weapon and left him bewildered.

***

With her audacious plans in motion, it became imperative that the West Witch erase all traces of Peter Myers. Madam Devow was not a believer in transmitting important or entrapping information over the telephone, therefore she summoned Glen Thompkins to the estate before dawn. Their conversation that morning became the only social engagement type of meeting they would ever had, as the bush doctor arranged for them to have tea on her rear verandah. During their brief meeting Madam Devow disclosed everything she had learned about Peter Myers, including where to locate the most convicting piece of evidence, which was his lost cell phone.

Glen was barely finished with his tea when he received the call to proceed to the murder scene behind the Burger King Restaurant, where an employee found the two male victims killed. By the time Officer Thompkins arrived on the scene, the entire area had been taped off and five of his colleagues from the Forensic Department were busy recovering evidence. The cellphone described by his spiritual advisor was in the exact location instructed, hence Glen recovered it and used Peter's phone to connect all the players involved. Peter's cellular was filled with pictures of his family and friends and most condemningly, proved that he spoke with the murdered victims only minutes before they were killed. All the evidence produced by Mama Devow helped to identify and forge a murder case against Peter Myers, who was unaware he had been scratched by one of his attacker's and dropped specs of blood at the scene, lost his phone during the scuffle and left his unique tire prints that could identify his Suzuki. To ensure that his team of vigilante officers performed the arrest, Glen methodically argued that the shooting was drug and gang related, thereby the V-Squad were assigned the task of bringing Peter Myers to justice.

Glen met the members of his Vanquish Squad team at their headquarters, which used to be a small garage used to repair police cruisers behind the main station. Despite the early time of the morning, the scent of Marijuana was prevalent when approaching the building, while inside, the team members smoked huge joints and drank Wray & Nephew Overproof White Rum, chased with water like it was coffee. The Vanquish Squad members were the only group of officers in the parish who did not follow the proper protocol of Law Enforcement, but, due to their crime efficiency, nobody complained. Thompkins first had to lower the volume on the radio to attract his peer's attention before he proceeded to brief them on their manhunt mission.

"Gentlemen… them identify the shooter who killed the two youths at the Burger King last night as one Peter Myers. Now it has become our duty to bring this dead man in for questioning, so get ready and let's go put him on ice," Glen instructed!

Three of the team members rode out on their individual motorbikes, while Glen and two others climbed into a Yukon SUV. Every member of the team was equipped with the latest technology in communications that allowed them to operate more professionally as a unit. The Squad members on motorbikes were the first to reach the wanted man's location and quietly positioned themselves around the house to ensure that no one escaped through windows or the back door. Glen and the other officers rode onto the scene once their comrades were in place and ran up to the front door. There was a locked security burglar bar gate ahead of the main door with which the officers had to contend, hence Officer Rogers used a lock cutter to severe the padlocks. With the locks disabled the officers slid open the barred gate and checked the lock at the door, which was also closed.

"Boom," Officer Barker kicked in the door at which his comrades charged into the residence!

"Police, we have a warrant for Peter Myers," Glen yelled!

There were three men and a woman inside the two-bedroom house, one of whom was Peter who was sound asleep, his brother Delroy My-

THE DEVIL'S CONCUBINE

ers, a friend named Rick Pierce and his girlfriend, Tania Steel. Delroy was the first male shot and killed while trying to run from the living room to alert his brother who was inside the bedroom. Tania was in the kitchen preparing breakfast for Rick and herself when the coppers charged in shooting at everybody and everything. Although the female managed to raise both her hands to illustrate her surrender, Officer Barker callously shot her in the sternum to eliminate all witnesses. As Tania fell to the ground, she overheard separate incidents of bullets being fired inside the house, after the first two Squad members to enter moved to both bedrooms and assassinated the men there. An unarmed Rick was shot twice in the chest while Glen emptied an entire magazine at Peter. Before exiting the house or alerting dispatch to send emergency paramedics, Vanquish Squad members planted weapons beside Delroy and Rick to justify their use of excessive force. Tania was believed to be dead until paramedics checked her and found a faint pulse, so she was rushed to the hospital with life threatening injuries, but fortunately died on route.

Chapter 18

Danielle began revealing signs of being pregnant weeks thereafter which began with the disruption to her menstruation cycle. For clarification that a baby should be expected, Barbara acquired and used a pregnancy test that revealed Danielle was indeed pregnant. Weeks of crying alone in silence and the constant thought of her mother getting shot in the head darkened the young captive's heart, but her determination to survive her prison and have her revenge consumed her. It took some time for Danielle to get comfortable being imprisoned in her own body, and the only thing that kept her sane was knowing she couldn't help herself unless she remained focused on the task ahead.

Dion always utilized the expertise of the members of her network for all her business interests, thus, for the next nine months Cynthia became

Danielle's personal pediatrician, and thus she ensured that there were no complications during the pregnancy. With Danielle being incapable of expressing her feelings, the Registered Nurse got assigned to visit and examine the expecting mother every evening after she finished her shift at the hospital.

When Cynthia got assigned to her temporary post, her first issues of concern had to do with Danielle's baby delivery, which would be impossible if the child's mother could not perform the required actions necessary for an actual childbirth. Mama Devow's response to Cynthia's concerns for Danielle and the unborn baby was that "she learnt the proper technique to perform a Cesarean operation," as the witch would consider no other options. Cynthia was also worried about how to explain returning home at a much later hour than normal to her husband, therein the West Witch gave her a magic potion for Herbert to drink that would cause him to become disinterested. During the next few months Cynthia partook in two Cesarean operations at the hospital where she even recorded the doctors' techniques, noted the drugs diagnosed to the patients and even read literatures on the procedure. With such an unprecedented case and zero tolerance for failure, Cynthia instructed Barbara from the beginning of the pregnancy "to check on Danielle regularly and alert her the instant she realized their patient's water had broken."

Madam Devow refused to divulge anything she knew about Danielle when, in fact, she was quite aware of the exact date on which the baby was to be born. The Devow female offspring all remarkably shared the same birthday, which was on the sixth of June, plus similar tattoos resembling birthmarks directly over their hearts. Barbara had lived with and served as the witch's maid for nearly 40 years, yet still she had absolutely no idea when her boss' birthday was or her exact age. Had it not been for their uncanny family resemblance, Barbara would have never assumed her employer could be related to Danielle, whom she had never seen before.

After administering Danielle's second injection one day, Barbara exited the room to find Dion standing at the opposite end of the lightly lit hallway. Mama Devow called to her and ordered her to "go by Mr. Lu's store and pick up her order," which had already been filled. Barbara went downstairs and informed the driver "they would be going to visit

MAMA DEVOW

the Chinaman's Herbal Shop," at which the chauffeur went and prepared the car. Madam Devow demanded absolute professionalism from her staff members, at all times and sexual relations were forbidden, therefore, business trips were quite boring without any form of radio entertainment or conversation. A trip to Mr. Lu's Herbal Remedies Store and back generally took an hour but there were massive delays due to road repairs along the roadway.

When they reached the herbal store, Barbara went in alone and left the driver inside the vehicle in front of the store. Sav-La-Mar and the surrounding areas had been suffering through a melting heatwave, therefore the soothing and cool temperature inside the genetic herbals establishment was welcomed. There were four customers ahead of Barbara who joined the line and patiently awaited her turn. After Mr. Lu served the next two customers a suspiciously behaving man walked in and looked around before he withdrew a Remington .380 Automatic handgun and waved it around at everyone. A female customer about to enter Mr. Lu's store noticed the gun-wielding thief inside and ran off to alert security. With everyone inside the store subdued, the armed thief ran behind the counter and demanded the storeowner passed over the money from the cash register? Mr. Lu wisely surrendered the money and did as instructed to avoid getting shot and killed by the desperate robber. Once the thief received the money, he began heading for the exit then shoved his weapon into his waist as he exited the store.

Dion's chauffeur observed the thief hiding his weapon and moved to step out of his vehicle, when suddenly a plain cloths gentleman who was walking towards the thief brandished a Spartan .45 within close range and shot him twice in the chest. The entire ordeal was indeed terrifying yet still the witch's chauffeur reacted as if it was of no consequence, as he walked past the commotion and rushed into the store to check if Barbara was alright. The man who shot the thief was undercover Detective Markus Dwyer of the Vanquish Squad, who was inside the patty shop a few doors down from Mr. Lu's when the female rushed in screaming, 'someone is robbing the Chinaman!' Mr. Lu despite being robbed by the assailant, brought out a white sheet for them to use and cover the body that was only a foot away from his business door.

By time the Crime Scene Investigators arrived, blocked off the area, collected evidence and statements from witnesses, watched Mr. Lu security video, removed their cruisers blocking the entrance and allow the victims to leave it was well into the evening. The West Witch's only appointment that evening was one of her regular palm-reading sessions, thus she was occupied with the client when the maid returned home. Barbara went directly to Madam Devow's private study and placed the package on her desk, but while checking the time on the clock Dion contacted her telepathically with instructions. The maid left the package and turned around and walked directly to the Reading Chamber, where she opened the door and guided the female client to the entrance.

"Where the hell you been all this time gal, is hours since you gone," Mama Devow declared?!

"I'm sorry Madam but somebody robbed Mr. Lu and was trying to---," Barbara began!

"Escape when an undercover officer killed," added Madam Devow finishing her sentence! "How long before our guest gets her next treatment?"

"In an hour and a half Ma'am… but I'm going to check on her right now. If you'll please excuse me," said Barbara?

Barbara then made her way up to the bedroom tier and turned on the lights as she walked into the room. The first thing that caught her attention was the huge puddle of water around Danielle's pelvic area therefore she went over and examined her. Danielle, who always had her eyes wide open stared maliciously at her, wherein she rushed out to notify those of interest. Barbara immediately advised Madam Devow that, "Danielle's water had broken, and her baby would be coming soon" before she contacted Cynthia and advised her of the developments.

The Emergency Ward at the Public Hospital was extremely busy that evening as a local shootout between two rival gangs produced several wounded victims. It had been an extremely busy and frustrating day for Cynthia's nursing crew, which was short staffed by two nurses who had called in sick that morning. An ambulance with two freshly wounded gangsters pulled up at the ER Entrance and Cynthia was rushing out with a gurney to collect one of the patients when Barbara telephoned her cell phone. Despite having a seriously injured man waiting for attention, Cynthia neglected her patient and advised the head nurse "there was a crisis at home" then abruptly left for the day. When leaving the ER Ward Cynthia overheard a nurse mention that the patient she ignored had died, but she was far more concerned about Danielle's and her personal safety.

Madam Devow brought an old magic book into her Private Study where Barbara left the packages from Mr. Lu on top of her desk. Before attending to the package, the witch opened the magic book to page 319, which was entitled, "Reinstatement Ceremony" and read all three requisites. Dion's intricate plot to remain the queen required that they kill Danielle exactly at midnight, at which time her inheritance would automatically get transferred to her daughter who was too young for the position; hence the Dark Magic power would revert to the Old Woman who would serve until the child came of age. The first requisite was for the assassination of three wasted souls who would suffer the persecution for Danielle in Hell, after she failed to uphold her family's legacy. While cutting away the tape on the box Dion telephoned Glen Thompkins who was in the midst of an interrogation.

Vanquish Squad members Delroy Pierce and Officer Thompkins were cruising around town when they saw a gang member wanted for questioning at a local tire store. The officers pulled up with guns drawn and detained the gangbanger and brought him into the business' toilet to search and interrogate. Glen jammed the nozzle of his gun inside a gangbanger's mouth and was threatening him for information, when his cellular rang at which he stopped the questioning and answered the phone. The thug being harassed closed his eyes and hoped the gun didn't discharge accidentally as the V-Squad Leader gently massaged the weapon's trigger while conversing.

"Good evening Ma'am, how may I be of service?"

"I need for you to come by the house around 11:30 tonight!"

"Yes, ma'am no problem!"

"And Glen one final thing… kill him!"

"Boom," exploded the firearm as Officer Thompkins unintentionally shot the man he had been interrogating, and was about to gather incriminating evidence from! Madam Devow smiled and hung up the phone as she opened the package and inspected its contents. Officer Delroy

Pierce, who was guarding the bathroom door while Glen antagonized the detainee, came running in with his gun at hand to check what had happened. Glen signaled everything was fine as he removed a small 22 caliber weapon from his pocket, grabbed the dead man's hand and coiled his fingers around the handle, to insinuate that the gangbanger pulled a gun and he killed him.

***

Cynthia arrived at the Devow estate 30 minutes later and received instructions from the West Witch on how to proceed, before she rushed up to Danielle's room. After examining the patient to ensure she was ready to give birth the nurse first gave Danielle an injection to help with the pain despite her paralyzed status, then placed an oxygen mask over her face to allow her to breath. An I.V with fluids was attached to Danielle arm, while Barbara brought in clean towels and warm water in a basin. While the epidural anesthesia numbed the pregnant woman's body, Cynthia had Barbara arrange the room for surgery as they prepared to remove the baby from the kidnapped victim's womb. Once Cynthia realized that the anesthesia had taken effect, she went to work by cleansing the area around which she would be cutting through the skin and made a six-inch incision with her scalpel. The registered nurse precisely followed the techniques she had learned and delivered Danielle's baby, as the mother watched with tears rolling down the side of her face.

The moment the little girl entered the world she cried out loud without the influence of anyone, hence her screams travelled to every corner of the house. Cynthia passed the child to Barbara for her to clean away the blood and mucus while she reinserted Danielle womb and began stapling together her stomach. The maid, who was normally reserved, had not handled a baby in many years, therefore she was extremely playful and delightful with the newly born baby. Barbara was unaware of what Cynthia was doing until she finished cleansing the child and turned around, at which she quickly stopped the nurse from finishing the surgery.

"What are you doing… didn't Madam Devow tell you not to sew her back up," argued Barbara?!

MAMA DEVOW

"Oh yeah, sorry I somehow forgot," responded Cynthia!

"Here… she told you to bring the child to her! You will find her down in her Spell Chamber," stated Barbara.

Cynthia removed the rubber gloves from her hands and the surgical clothes she operated in before she took the baby from Barbara and left the room. In her absence, the maid started gathering the bloodied linens and towels and threw them into a pillowcase to bring to the laundry. With all the excitement, Barbara forgot to give Danielle her next prescribed injection and went about the room moping the floor and cleaning the dresser and night tables. Danielle began regaining sensation in her joints and slowly twitched her fingers and toes, but most appreciatively closed her eye lids which had been wide open since the day Cynthia drugged her.

Barbara walked over to the night table to the right of the bed and began cleaning it during which she looked over at Danielle and speculated that she might be dead, having never seen her in such a state. Suddenly the paralyzed captive opened her eyes and reached over and grabbed onto the maid's hand, which almost caused her to faint under the exhaustion. The successor to the Devow Empire pierced through Barbara's soul with a condemning stare that went beyond Dion's control and totally reformed the house servant.

"Yes, from this moment I will obey only you Madam Danielle Devow," declared Barbara once the captive released her hand, at which she took the nurse's position and finished what Cynthia had started!

***

When descending the stairs with the baby, Cynthia heard a knock at the front entrance and, knowing the maid was indisposed, she attended to the door. Both visitors acknowledged each other having worked together before, following which Cynthia walked away and left Detective Thompkins to close the door.

"Can you please inform Madam Devow that I am here," Glen asked?

THE DEVIL'S CONCUBINE

"Do I look like the maid to you? Come man I think she inside her Spell Chamber," Cynthia declared!

The registered nurse turned her head for a second to respond to the visiting officer and, when she spun back around, the West Witch was miraculously standing directly in front of her. Dion held aloft both hands indicating she wanted the infant, to which Cynthia gracious handed her the newborn.

"You have done well, you may go," instructed Dion without so much as a thank you for your services!

Glen held the door open for Cynthia who grabbed her purse and politely bowed in respect before leaving the dwelling. The West Witch had a mean and unfriendly demeanor and remained true to form even when dealing with the newest member in her family. Detective Thompkins followed Madam Devow to her study where she sat the infant down in a baby rocker, and walked over to a wooden carved box that sat alone on a corner table, opened the lid and removed a bronze handled dagger. Dion held the dagger flat across both hands and brought it over the Glen and gave it to him.

"As the clock strike midnight, I want you to plunge this dagger into the heart of the girl you brought to me," Dion instructed!

Glen looked at the time on his watch and the clock on her wall and noted they were synchronized at which he answered. "Whatever you wish Ma'am!"

While the West Witch brought the baby into her Spell Chamber where she had everything arranged for the Reinstatement Ceremony, Glen utilized the precious few minutes left before his appointment to fix and consume two shots of his favorite rum from the witch's personal bar. Once inside the Spell Chamber Mama Devow locked the door behind them and placed the naked infant on a blanket in the center of the Circle of Realms carved into the floor. The only lighting inside the room came from six lit candles each of which were placed at a specific point around the circle.

The Nyabinghi Drummer began beating an ancient Spiritual African Tribunal beat meant to request the presence of the Governing Spirit Forces that established the Obeah Religion. Dion lit six incense sticks she retrieved from the parcel sent by Mr. Lu and walked around the room humming like a Buddhist with her eyes closed until 11:55 P.M. The Witch then stopped at the top of the circle and bowed her head in submission while mumbling a prayer to her God. Following the prayer, Madam Devow threw off her robe revealing her nude wrinkled body, as she began sprinkling Diamond Dust that was produced in mines of Africa, all around the room from inside the circle. As the clock approached midnight, the entire flooring outside the Circle of Realms disappeared, revealing the burning trenches and lava filled pits of the Underworld. The West Indies most revered Obeah woman could see the spirits she summoned rising from the depths of Hell to attend her coronation. Thus, all that was left was for Danielle to cease breathing.

The Detective slowly made his way up the stairs to Danielle's room and entered to find Barbara kneeling in the corner like a toddler on timeout punishment. Danielle had just finished dressing herself in one of Dion's sexy black dresses and was admiring herself in the dresser mirror when Glen appeared at the door holding the dagger. Detective Executioner peeked at his watch and noted the time had arrived to fulfill Dion's request, hence, he charged the recently recovered female with his dagger held high. The heir to the Devow Estate spun around before the detective drove the blade into her and stared Glen directly in the eyes, at which he froze like a brick of ice.

"If you weren't such a valuable commodity to my master, I burn you to ashes! Get out of mi house now!"

Glen's eyes filled with tears and leaked blood as he trembled and sincerely tried apologizing. "Sorry ma'am, I didn't know you are!"

At that Glen dropped the dagger and ran faster than he had ever ran to exit the house. Danielle picked up the dagger and slowly walked downstairs where the witch was locked inside her Spell Chamber. It was forbidden to open the door to the chamber whenever a ceremony was in process, as there stood the chance of evil spirits escaping back into the world. Despite knowing all this, Danielle who had been in a trancelike state since she recovered from the drugs, busted into the Spell Chamber while Dion was locked deep in meditation. The immense force that generated around Danielle created a blockage at the entrance that prevented anything from escaping. The incumbent witch was waiting for the glori-

THE DEVIL'S CONCUBINE

fication of being the next anointed queen with the killing of her successor, when, as if in a dream, she vividly saw Danielle floating towards her. To kill a witch in the state of meditation meant eternal damnation for her soul, therefore Danielle glided across the floor to Dion and grabbed the frail old woman around her neck with one hand.

"You killed everyone that I truly loved… Rot in Hell you, old bitch! This is for my mother," Danielle exclaimed as she pierced the knife into Dion's chest and withdrew it!

"Ahhh," screamed Dion continuously once she realized her condemned fate!

"This is for Mr. Kensington," said Danielle as she stabbed her again in the chest!

"This is for Kimberly," added Danielle with another stab to Dion's chest!

"This is for Jervais," again another stab!

"This is for Mrs. Kensington," again another stab!

"And this is for me Bitch," Danielle pierced the blade directly through the Obeah woman's heart and left the blade there permanently!

Dion had absolutely no idea how Danielle was able to survive the mental depression she expected would destroy her, therefore she fought with the demons that came to drag her into the Underworld. After killing the West Witch, Danielle picked up her child off the floor and wrapped her in the blanket and hugged her tightly inside the Circle of Realms, while the magical powers intended to anoint the Obeah Queen rained down on her.

Chapter 19

Deloris Devow and the mystery man Danielle caught her dealing with at the Kensington's house flew to Jamaica two days before Dion's Reinstatement Ceremony. The two Canadians spent the majority of their time in Montego Bay, where Deloris believed the West Witch could not detect her presence on the island. Between the time they landed and the date of the ceremony, both tourists went to three separate arms dealers in search of a long-range high-powered sniper rifle that came equipped with a night scope. They eventually purchased a Barrett M107 A1 Sniper Rifle that would offer them the opportunity to strike their target from long range, which was the only chance they stood at having any success. For the bullets to strike with righteousness, Deloris went to pray in a local church and secretly washed them in a tub of Holy Water.

THE DEVIL'S CONCUBINE

Danielle's grandmother planned on terminating their family's contract with the Devil regardless of who became the next Obeah Queen, therefore she did not travel back to the land of her birth simply to perform a rescue operation. The man she travelled with was Renald St. Justine, a paid mercenary, who used to be the most accurate long-range shooter in the Canadian army. Deloris had spent the majority of her years in Canada researching her family history in order to find a solution to their dilemma, which she tried on several occasions by attempting to baptize Danielle. The heir to the Obeah Queen's Throne would never know how close Deloris came to killing her that final day at the Kensington's while she slept, but her grandmother's love for her prevented the baptized Christian from taking her life. Following the killings of the Kensington's and her beloved daughter, Deloris realized the only way to put a stop to the curse was by killing everyone of her family members involved in sorcery, which was why she travelled back to the one place in the world she had vowed to never again visit.

Mercenary for hire were killers who typically worked alone, but being in the kill zone was a stipulation implemented by their employer. Deloris paid Renald $20,000.00 to assassinate whoever became the next Obeah Queen, but she was not about to sit home and wait for a telephone confirmation. Even though the hired assassin didn't care about whoever was at the other end of his weapon, the uncanny resemblance between the Devow ladies compelled him to ask, "why Deloris wanted her relative dead?" Renald had learnt from his background check of his female employer that she was a devoted church member, but her outlandish story about magic spells and witchcraft had him convinced she suffered with mental disability.

Dusk had fallen by the time Deloris and Renald got to Savanna la Mar, so they drove directly to the Devow Estate. Even though Deloris showed face by acting as if she was not nervous to avoid deterring the mercenary, she was terrified beyond mention, knowing exactly who they were going up against. Deloris believed Dion would continue her reign and thus advised the sharpshooter that "the designated queen would have to bring the newborn heir out onto the back porch and raise her up to the full moon." To complete the Reinstatement Ceremony, the child would have to be shone upon by the full moon, following which neither the baby nor the witch would leave the house for three straight months, thus that would be their only opportune time to kill her. They parked their rented vehicle at a distance and snuck onto the property where Renald selected a vantage point from which he could get a clear shot.

The West Witch had a huge chicken coop approximately 150 yards from the main house where she raised chickens for profit. Ten yards to the right of the coop was a tree stump from which the mercenary planned to execute his target. Deloris argued that "she believed they would be much safer behind the chicken coop", but the professional marksman who thought she over-exaggerated the truth about her family, decided otherwise. Behind the camouflage of trees and bushes both assassins laid down on the ground and waited patiently for their one opportunity, which came hours later at 12:13 A.M.

By the time the newly crowned Obeah Queen walked out onto the porch Renald had dozed off but kept his weapon in position to fire. Deloris watched a cloaked female walk out with the baby at hand and felt a warmness knowing the child came from Danielle, but she could not clearly see that far and had no idea who the woman was. After watching them both for a few seconds, Deloris woke Renald and advised him "the target had emerged!" The Mercenary prepared himself and looked at his target through the night scope and was about to shoot the woman in the head when Deloris held him on the arm and stopped him and asked, "who is that my granddaughter?" Renald's response shocked Deloris who gasped a huge sigh knowing it was her beloved Danielle, but then she released a hold of him signaling her approval to shoot.

The hired mercenary took another look through his night scope and repositioned Danielle's forehead in the center, but the newly crowned Obeah Queen unexplainably had her eyes plastered on him. Danielle looked at Renald with her paralyzing stare, at which he tried to pull the trigger but could not move his finger. Hence, with her left hand securely holding her infant, the witch motioned as if she was scratching herself across her face and eyes with her right hand. Renald was instantly blinded and accidentally discharged his weapon as he yanked his hands away to cover his eyes, then rolled about the ground screaming in pain.

"Ahhh my eyes... my eyes... I can't see! Help me, I'm blind I can't see," Renald screamed!

The Mercenary had visible scratch marks across his face and eyeballs and was unexplainably blinded by the new Obeah Queen. Deloris could not see the female clearly, but she was certain that the bullet missed its intended target as Danielle was still standing with her daughter at hand. At the realization that they had failed, Deloris went temporarily insane and picked up the huge rifle then started walking towards her granddaughter. To ensure her grandmother did not get off a lucky shot, Danielle cast a spell by waving her hand before her face and said, "cloud vision," at which Deloris' sight became unimaginably blurry.

The Jamaican defector was no gun expert, nor had she ever fired a weapon, but she had observed Renald handle the rifle long enough to know how to reload, point and shoot. With her first bullet selected Deloris fired the shot at both her grand and great-granddaughters, but Danielle didn't flinch or attempt to run away. There were five bullets inside of the rifle when Deloris lost all sense of reasoning and began making a charge at her siblings. Four bullets later she had gotten within 15 yards of the targets and held the rifle sturdy as she fired the last shot, which totally missed Danielle and shattered a flowerpot on the porch.

"Please… no more of this life Lord! Please," Deloris pled as she fell to her knees!

"Old woman you lucky that I used to have love for you once, or I rip out your heart where you stand for your insolence! You, your Lord, and your friend have five minutes to get off my property! I suggest you be gone way before that, and don't ever let me see you again," threatened Danielle, who turned and walked into her house with her daughter and slammed the door!

The End

MAMA DEVOW

Special Recognition

Edited by
Joel Saibel

Cover Pictures by
Clyde Williams
ccwdesign@hotmail.com

Book Design by
Jim Bisakowski
Bookdesign@shaw.ca

THE DEVIL'S CONCUBINE

Rhoan Flowers' Previous Novels

Informer 1/The Wars of Men

Yahweh

Informer 2/The Treachery of Friends

The Blue Jay And The Squirrel

MAMA DEVOW

THE DEVIL'S CONCUBINE

MAMA DEVOW

www.ingramcontent.com/pod-product-compliance
Lightning Source LLC
Chambersburg PA
CBHW071450070526
44578CB00001B/290